# An Arkful of
# ANIMAL
# JOKES
## FOR KIDS!

# An Arkful of
# ANIMAL
# JOKES
## FOR KIDS!

## SHILOH kidz

An Imprint of Barbour Publishing, Inc.

© 2020 by Barbour Publishing, Inc.

ISBN 978-1-64352-251-7

Published by Shiloh Kidz, an imprint of Barbour Publishing, Inc., 1810 Barbour Drive, Uhrichsville, Ohio 44683, www.shilohkidz.com

*Our mission is to inspire the world with the life-changing message of the Bible.*

Member of the
Evangelical Christian
Publishers Association

Printed in the United States of America.
000101  1219  BP

# Contents

# Introduction

Greetings, my friend—I am Noah, keeper of the world's first floating zoo. A fun job, you think? Forget it! Talk about stress—there's only eight of us humans to keep thousands of seasick critters in line. Every day, we have to feed them, listen to them asking "are we there yet?", and keep the cockroaches and woodpeckers from eating through the walls of the boat. It's enough to wear out a man half my age. . .you know, one of those three-hundred-year-old whippersnappers.

Of course, humor's been the key to keeping my sanity, and I've had plenty of material to draw from. I've got stories of skunks, snakes, and snails. I've got tales ("tails," get it?) of dogs, deer, and dinosaurs. I've got jokes about chickens, mice, gorillas, and every other conceivable creature.

Maybe you'd enjoy hearing my routine. . .the owls tell me it's a hoot.

So come on board. Just watch where you step, and don't make any loud noises or sudden movements. Relax for a while and enjoy *An Arkful of Animal Jokes—for Kids*!

# Alligators

What do you call a sick alligator?
*An illigator.*

.................................................

What do you get if you cross an alligator with a flower?
*I don't know, but I'm not going to smell it.*

.................................................

There was once a lazy alligator that roamed the banks of the river. Whenever a boat passed him, those onboard would be sure to keep their hands inside the vessel, because it was known that he was always looking for a handout.

.................................................

What do you get if you cross a snowman with an alligator?
*Frostbite.*

Once there was a millionaire who had a collection of alligators. He kept them in the pool behind his mansion. The millionaire also had a very beautiful daughter who was single. One day he decided to throw a huge party, and during the course of the party he announced, "Ladies and gentlemen, I have a proposition for every man here: I will give one million dollars or my daughter to the man who can swim across this pool full of alligators and emerge alive!"

As soon as he finished his proclamation, there was a large splash. A man was in the pool, swimming with all his might and screaming in fear. The crowd cheered him on as he crashed through the water. Finally, he jumped out on the other side with only a torn shirt and several minor injuries. The millionaire was awestruck.

He said, "Sir, that was amazing! I didn't think it could be done! But I must keep my end of the bargain.

Do you want my daughter or the one million dollars?"

The guy answered, "I don't want your money or your daughter. I just want the person who pushed me into the water!"

# Ants

Where do ants go on vacation?
   *Frants.*

..................................................

What do you call a one-hundred-year-old ant?
   *An antique.*

..................................................

Teacher: "Boys and girls, there is a wonderful example in the life of the ant. Every day the ant goes to work and works all day long. Every day the ant is busy. And in the end, what happens?"
   Johnny: "Someone steps on him."

..................................................

What kind of ant is good at math?
   *An account-ant.*

A bad golfer cringed when his drive landed on an anthill. Choosing a sand wedge, he positioned himself and swung at the half-buried ball. Sand and ants flew. The ball hadn't moved.

Again the golfer braced and swung. Again the anthill was devastated, but the ball lay unmoved.

Inside the panic-stricken ant colony, one ant yelled to his friend, "Come on! That big white ball seems to be a pretty safe place!"

# Bears

Where do polar bears like to vacation?
*Brrrr-muda.*

...................................................

What time is it when five grizzly bears chase you?
*Five after one.*

...................................................

What do you call a grizzly bear with no teeth?
*A gummy bear.*

...................................................

How do bears walk around?
*With bear feet.*

Bob: "I thought you were going bear hunting!"

Bill: "I was. But I only made it as far as the highway."

Bob: "What happened?"

Bill: "Well, I saw a road sign that said Bear Left, so I came home!"

......................................................

Hunter 1: "Look! Here's some bear tracks!"

Hunter 2: "Great. I'll go see where he came from, and you go see where he went."

......................................................

What is a bear's favorite drink?
*Coca-Koala.*

......................................................

Two men went out to hunt bear. On opening morning, a light snow fell, and one stayed in the cabin while the other went out hunting. He soon found a huge grizzly and shot at it, but merely wounded it. The infuriated bear charged toward him. He dropped his rifle and started running for the cabin as fast as he could. He ran fast, but the bear was just a little faster, gaining on him with every step. Just as he reached the open cabin door, he tripped and fell. Too close behind to stop, the bear tripped over him and went rolling into the cabin.

The man jumped up, closed the cabin door, and yelled to his friend inside, "You skin this one, and I'll go get another one!"

......................................

What do you call a crybaby bear?
*Whiny the Pooh.*

......................................

Two easterners were hunting in the Rocky Mountain wilderness when a huge grizzly bear sprang onto their path, reared up, and roared.

One hunter was terrified. The other kept his presence of mind and calmly instructed, "Don't move a muscle. Just stand like a statue, and the bear will get bored and go away."

"H–h–how do you know?"

"I read it in a book about the Lewis and Clark expedition."

They both stood motionless. The bear didn't go away but instead drew closer and roared more furiously.

The first hunter stammered, "I–I–I think the bear must've read the same book!"

.................................................

Where do polar bears vote?
*The North Poll.*

.................................................

What do Paddington Bear and Winnie the Pooh pack for their holidays?
*The bear essentials.*

.................................................

It's a sunny morning in the big forest and the Bear family is just waking up. Baby Bear goes downstairs and sits in his small chair at the table. He looks into his small bowl. It's empty!

"Who's been eating my porridge?" he squeaks. Daddy Bear comes to the table and sits in his big chair. He looks into his big bowl. It's also empty!

"Who's been eating my porridge?" he roars.

Mommy Bear calls from the kitchen, "How many times do we have to go through this? It was Mommy Bear who got up first. It was Mommy Bear who woke everybody up. It was Mommy Bear who unloaded the dishwasher. It was Mommy Bear who went out to get the newspaper. It was Mommy Bear who set the table. It was Mommy Bear who put the cat out, cleaned the litter box, and filled the cat's water and food dish. And now that you've finally decided to come downstairs and start your day, listen well because I'm only going to say this one time—I haven't had time to make the porridge yet!"

What do you get if you cross a grizzly bear and a harp?

*A bear-faced lyre.*

Two campers are hiking in the woods when suddenly a bear starts chasing them.

Both campers start running for their lives, when one of them stops and starts to put on his running shoes.

His buddy says, "What are you doing? You can't outrun a bear!"

His friend replies, "I don't have to outrun the bear, I only have to out-run you!"

# Bees

What kind of bee is always dropping the football?
*A fumblebee.*

What do you call a bee that hums very quietly?
*A mumblebee.*

Why do bees hum?
*Because they can't remember the words.*

What is another name for a bunch of bees?
*A pretty good report card.*

How does a bee get to school?
*It takes the buzz.*

What do bees do with the honey they make?
*Cell it.*

What goes ZZUB, ZZUB, ZZUB?
*A bee flying backward.*

What do bees do if they want to use public transport?
*Wait at a buzz stop.*

What does a bee get at McDonald's?
*A humburger.*

What do you get if you cross a bee with a doorbell?
*A hum dinger.*

# Birds, Domestic

Gary showed off his singing parrot to his friend Ken.

"If you pull his right leg, he'll sing 'Happy Birthday,'" said Gary. "And if you pull his left leg, he'll sing 'The Star-Spangled Banner.'"

"What happens if you pull both legs?" Ken asked.

"Squawk!" said the parrot. "I'd fall off the perch!"

.................................................

A woman went to the pet shop to buy a parrot. When she picked out a rare breed, the owner congratulated her on her choice.

"If you'd like, I could send you the bill at the end of the month," said the pet shop owner.

"No, thanks," said the woman, "I'd like to take the whole bird today."

..................................................

A man bought a parrot, and for twenty years the bird was silent, never uttering so much as a word. Every morning the parrot would wake up, stand patiently on its perch, and wait for its owner to come and feed it.

One morning, the man overslept. Using its beak, the parrot pried the cage door open, flew out, and perched on the man's head.

Pecking its owner's nose, the parrot squawked and said, "Excuse me, but it's nearly noon and I'm starving."

The man sat upright. "Polly, you can talk!"

"Of course I can talk," said the parrot.

"Then why haven't you said anything for twenty years?" asked the man.

"Because up until now," replied the bird, "the service has been excellent."

..................................................

A lady goes into a pet store. "I'm quite lonely," she says to the clerk. "I need a pet to keep me company."

"Well," replies the clerk, "how about this nice parrot? He'll talk to you."

"That's just what I need," says the lady. She buys the parrot and takes him home. The next day the lady comes back to the pet store. "That parrot isn't talking to me yet," she says.

"Hmm, let's see," says the clerk. "I know! You can buy this little ladder for his cage. He'll climb the ladder, and then he'll talk." So she heads home with a newly purchased ladder. The next day she comes back again.

"Hey, that parrot still hasn't said a word," she says to the pet store clerk.

He thinks a minute. "How about this little mirror?" he says. "You hang it at the top of the ladder. The parrot will climb the ladder, look in the mirror, and then he'll talk to you."

"Okay," she says and buys the mirror and goes home. But the next day the lady is back in the shop.

"I must admit, I'm getting a bit discouraged," she says. "That parrot still won't talk to me."

The clerk scratches his head. "Let me think. Here—try this bell. You hang it over the mirror. The parrot will climb the ladder, look in the mirror, ring the bell, and then he will surely talk to you!"

"All right, I'll give it a try," says the lady. And she buys the bell and takes it home. The next day the same lady comes back to the pet shop, and she is very distressed.

"What's wrong?" asks the clerk.

"My parrot. . .well, he died," she answers sadly.

"Oh no! I'm so sorry for your loss!" exclaims the clerk. "But I must ask you, did the parrot ever say anything to you?"

"Oh yes, he did say one thing, right before he died," she replies.

"Well, what did he say?" asks the clerk.

The lady replies, "He said, 'Doesn't that store carry any food?' "

......................................

David got a parrot for his birthday. The parrot was fully grown with a bad attitude and a rude vocabulary. So David tried very hard to change the bird's manners. He would always say polite words, play soft music— anything he could think of to set a good example—but nothing worked.

David was really frustrated. He yelled at the bird, and the bird got worse. He shook the bird, and the bird got angrier and even more rude.

One day, David felt so desperate that he picked the parrot up and put it in the freezer. For a few moments he heard the bird squawking and flapping; then suddenly everything was quiet. David was worried that he might have hurt the parrot and quickly opened the freezer door. The bird calmly stepped out onto David's arm and said, "I am so sorry that I have offended you with my language and actions, and I beg your forgiveness. I will try to correct my behavior."

David was amazed at the change in the bird and was about to ask what had caused it when the parrot continued, "May I ask what the chicken did?"

.................................................

A lady went to a pet shop. "I would like to buy two yellow canaries," she told the owner.

"I'm sorry," the owner replied. "We don't have any canaries, but we have these"—showing her some pale green parakeets.

"That isn't what I'm looking for," the lady stated.

But the persistent pet store owner refused to give up. He said, "Just think of them as yellow canaries that aren't quite ripe yet."

........................................

A pastor and a deacon visited a house to call on a parishioner. They knocked, and a small voice replied, "Come in."

They went in, but although they found no one there, they did find two big Doberman dogs.

The churchmen called out nervously, "Hello, is anyone here?" and the voice of a little old lady said, "Come in."

It sounded like it was coming from the kitchen, so they walked gently in that direction before the narrowed eyes of the two dogs. The men came upon a parrot, which was repeatedly saying, "Come in, come in, come in. . ."

Exhaling, the pastor said, "You silly old parrot, is that all you can say?"

With the same small voice the parrot said, "Sic 'em."

A wealthy man paid twenty-five thousand dollars for an exotic bird for his mother.

"How did you like the bird?" he asked her later.

She responded, "It was delicious."

...................................................

A lady was walking past a pet store when a parrot said, "Hey, lady! That's an ugly dress you're wearing!" The lady was angry but continued on her way.

On the way home, she passed by the pet store again, and the parrot once more said, "Hey, lady! That's an ugly dress you're wearing!" She was enraged now, so she went into the store and said that she wanted the bird disposed of. The store manager apologized profusely and promised he would make sure the parrot didn't say it again.

The next day, she deliberately passed by the store to test the parrot. "Hey, lady!" it said.

"Yes?"

"You know."

....................................................

Mrs. Peterson phoned the repairman because her dishwasher had stopped working. He couldn't accommodate her with an "after-hours" appointment, and since she had to go to work, she told him, "I'll leave the key under the doormat. Please repair the dishwasher, leave the bill on the counter, and I will mail you a check. By the way, I have a large rottweiler inside named Killer. He won't bother you. I also have a parrot, and whatever you do, make certain you do not talk to the bird!"

Well, sure enough the dog, Killer, totally ignored the repairman, but the whole time he was there, the parrot yelled and screamed, driving him crazy.

As he was ready to leave, he just couldn't help himself. He looked at the bird and said, "You have annoyed me all morning. Be quiet!"

To which the bird replied, "Killer, get him!"

......................................................

A lady was expecting the plumber; he was supposed to come at ten o'clock. Ten o'clock came and went— no plumber. Eleven o'clock, twelve o'clock, one o'clock—no plumber. She concluded he wasn't coming and went out to do some errands. While she was gone, the plumber arrived. He knocked on the door. The woman's parrot, in a cage by the door, asked, "Who is it?"

He replied, "It's the plumber."

The man stood waiting for the lady to let him in. When she didn't, he knocked again, and again the parrot said, "Who is it?"

He said, "It's the plumber!"

He waited, and again the lady didn't come to let him in. He knocked again, and again the parrot said, "Who is it?"

He said, "It's the plumber!"

Again he waited; again she didn't come. Again he knocked; again the parrot said, "Who is it?"

"Aarrrggghhh!" he said. In frustration, he banged his head against the door, which caused him to pass out and fall in the doorway.

The lady came home from her errands, only to see a man lying at the door. "Who is it?" she wondered out loud.

The parrot said, "It's the plumber."

..................................................

A man went to an auction. While there, he decided to bid on a parrot. He really wanted this bird, and he got caught up in the bidding. He kept increasing the bid, but kept getting outbid, so he bid higher and higher. Finally, after he bid much higher than he intended, he won the bid, and the parrot was his at last!

As he was paying for the bird, he said to the auctioneer, "I certainly hope this parrot can talk. I would be devastated to have paid this much for it, only to find out that he isn't able to talk!"

"Oh, he can, for sure," said the auctioneer. "Who do you think kept bidding against you?"

......................................

What do you get when a canary gets caught in a lawn mower?
*Shredded tweet.*

......................................

On reaching his plane seat, a man was taken aback to see a parrot strapped in the seat next to his. After regaining his wits, the man asked the flight attendant for a cup of coffee. Immediately, the parrot squawked, "And get me a chocolate milk, now!" The stewardess, flustered, brought back a chocolate milk for the parrot but forgot all about the coffee.

The man reminded her of the coffee, while the parrot emptied its glass and squawked, "And get me another chocolate milk, you slowpoke."

Upset, the poor girl came back shaking, carrying another chocolate milk—but no coffee.

Unaccustomed to such poor service, the man tried the parrot's approach. "I've asked you twice for a coffee. Go and get it now, or I'll make sure you lose your job!"

In an instant, two security guards grabbed both the man and the parrot and threw them out of the emergency exit.

As they plunged toward the ground, the parrot turned to the man and said, "For someone who can't fly, you've sure got an attitude."

...................................................

A young magician started to work on a cruise ship with his pet parrot. The parrot would always mess up his act by saying things like, "The card was up his sleeve!" or "The dove was in his pocket!"

One day the ship sank, and the magician and the parrot found themselves adrift, alone on a lifeboat. For a couple of days, they just sat there looking at each other. Finally, the parrot broke the silence and said, "Okay, I give up. What did you do with the ship?"

# Birds, Wild

What is an owl's favorite mystery?
*A whooo-dunit.*

How do baby birds learn to fly?
*They wing it.*

What do you get when you put five
ducks in a cardboard container?
*A box of quackers.*

What should you do when someone
throws a goose at you?
*Duck.*

What do you say when someone
throws a duck at a duck?
*"Duck, duck!"*

What do you say when someone throws a goose at a duck?
*"Duck, duck, goose!"*

..................................................

Show me an owl with laryngitis, and I'll show you a bird that doesn't give a hoot.

..................................................

Why did the stork stand on one leg?
*Because if he lifted the other leg, he'd fall.*

..................................................

A duck waddled into a country grocery store and asked the clerk, "Do you sell duck food here?"

"Of course not," replied the clerk. "We sell groceries to people, not ducks."

The next day, the duck returned and asked again, "Do you sell duck food?"

Annoyed, the clerk snapped, "No! No duck food."

When the duck returned the next day and posed the same question, the clerk threatened, "I've told you this is a grocery store for people, not birds. If you ever come back in here and ask me that question again, I will nail one of your webbed feet to the floor and laugh while you walk around in circles."

The next day the duck was back. "Do you sell nails?"

The clerk, out of patience, retorted, "Certainly not. This is a grocery store, not a hardware store."

The duck then asked, "Do you sell duck food?"

..................................................

Why wouldn't the duck go to the duck doctor?

*Because he was a quack.*

..................................................

Why do birds fly south for the winter?

*Because it's too far to walk.*

..................................................

How many penguins does it take to fly an airplane?

*None. Penguins can't fly.*

Which bird is always out of breath?
*A puffin.*

...............................................

What do you call a penguin in the desert?
*Lost.*

...............................................

What kind of bird does construction work?
*The crane.*

...............................................

Fred: "Someone said that you look like an owl."
Meg: "Who?"
Fred: "You sound like one too."

...............................................

What do you call a seagull when it flies over the bay?
*A bagel.*

...............................................

What does an educated owl say?
*Whom.*

...............................................

Two robins were sitting in a tree. "I'm really hungry," said the first one.

"Me too," said the second. "Let's fly down and find some lunch." They flew to the ground and found a nice plot of plowed ground full of worms. They ate and ate until they couldn't eat any more.

"I'm so full I don't think I'll be able to fly back up to the tree," said the first one.

"Me either. Let's just lie here and bask in the warm sun," said the second.

"Okay," said the first. They plopped down, basking in the sun. No sooner had they fallen asleep than a big fat tomcat snuck up and gobbled them up.

As he sat licking his paws after his meal, he thought, *I love baskin' robins.*

A little hatchling fell out of its nest and went crashing through the branches of the elm tree toward the ground.

"Are you all right?" called out a

robin as the chick went hurtling past his perch.

"So far!" said the little bird.

........................................

How did the exhausted sparrow land safely?

*By sparrowchute.*

........................................

What do ducks like on television?

*Duckumentaries.*

........................................

What is the most common illness in birds?

*Flu.*

........................................

What birds spend all their time on their knees?

*Birds of pray.*

........................................

Where do birds invest their money?

*In the stork market.*

........................................

Did you hear the story about the peacock that crossed the road?

*It is really a colorful tail. . . .*

# Bugs and Insects

Why did the firefly do well on the test?

*Because it was very bright.*

....................................................

What did the policeman say to the firefly?

*"Halt! Who glows there?"*

....................................................

Teacher: "If there are a dozen flies on the table and you swat one, how many are left?"

Student: "Uh, just the dead one?"

....................................................

Ron went into a drugstore and purchased a box of mothballs. The next day he returned and bought a second box. When he came back the third day, the clerk was quite curious, and he commented, "You sure must have lots of moths in your house!"

"Yes, I do," admitted Ron, "and I can't take it anymore. I've been throwing these balls at them for two days, and I haven't been able to hit a single one!"

........................................

"Are caterpillars good to eat?" asked a little boy at the dinner table.

"No," said his father. "Why would you ask a question like that?"

"Well, there was one in your salad, but it's gone now."

........................................

Why did the fly fly?
*Because the spider spied her.*

........................................

What is the insect's favorite game?
*Cricket.*

........................................

Why was the centipede dropped from the insect football team?
*He took too long to put his cleats on.*

What is green and can jump a mile in a minute?

*A grasshopper with hiccups.*

Why didn't the fly go near the computer?

*Because he was afraid to get caught in the web.*

The furious customer called the waitress over to his table and demanded to know what was in his soup.

She looked and shyly said, "I'll have to call the boss; I don't know one insect from another."

What do you call a nervous insect?

*Jitterbug.*

Two caterpillars were crawling along a twig when a butterfly flew by. "You know," said one caterpillar to the other, "you would never catch me up in one of those things."

A cricket walked into a London sporting goods store.

"Hey," said the clerk, shocked to see an insect with an interest in sports. "We have a game named after you."

"Really?" said the cricket. "You have a game called Charles?"

# Cats, Domestic

What happened to the cat that swallowed a ball of wool?
*It had mittens.*

What is a cat's favorite kind of computer?
*A laptop.*

What do you call an overweight cat?
*A flabby tabby.*

When Carl went away on vacation, his brother Ben promised to take care of his cat. The next day, Carl called Ben to see how the animal was doing.

"Your cat is dead," said Ben, matter-of-factly.

"Dead?" said the stunned Carl. "Why did you have to tell me like that?"

"How should I have told you?" asked Ben.

"Well," said Carl, "the first time I called, you could have broken it to me gently. You could have said my cat was on the roof, but the fire department was getting her down. The second time I called, you could have told me the cat fell out of the fireman's arms and broke its neck. The third time I called, you could have said that the vet did everything he could, but Fluffy passed away. That way it wouldn't have been so hard on me."

"I'm sorry," said Ben.

"That's all right. By the way, how's Mother?"

"She's up on the roof. . . ," said Ben.

What did the cat get on the test?

*A purr-fect score.*

........................................

What do you get when you put a kitten in a scanner?

*A copycat.*

........................................

What do cats drink on hot summer afternoons?

*Mice tea.*

........................................

Why did the cat family move next door to the mouse family?

*So they could have the neighbors for dinner.*

........................................

What do you call a cat that sings opera?

*Mewsical.*

........................................

What's the difference between a cat and a comma?

*One has the paws before the claws, and the other has the clause before the pause.*

Why was the cat afraid of the tree?
*He didn't like its bark.*

...................................................

If ten cats are on a boat and one jumps off, how many are left?
*None—they're all copycats.*

...................................................

Why was the cat so small?
*Because it only drank condensed milk.*

...................................................

A famous art collector was strolling through the city when he noticed a mangy cat drinking milk from a saucer in the doorway of a store.

He did a double take, as he observed that the saucer was quite rare and very valuable. He walked casually into the store and offered to buy the cat for two dollars. The store owner replied, "I'm sorry, but the cat is not for sale."

The collector persisted, saying, "Please, I need a hungry cat around the house to catch mice. I'll pay you twenty-five dollars for the cat."

The owner said, "Sold," and handed over the cat.

The collector continued, "For the twenty-five dollars, could you throw in the saucer too? I'm sure the cat is used to it, and I won't have to purchase a dish for her."

The owner replied, "Sorry, pal, but that is my lucky saucer. So far this week I've sold fifty-nine cats."

........................................................

A couple was going out for the evening to celebrate their anniversary. While they were getting ready, the husband put the cat outside. The taxi arrived, and as the couple walked out the door, the cat shot back into the house.

Not wanting their pet to have the run of the house while they were out, the husband went back upstairs to get the cat.

The wife didn't want it known that there would be no one home, so she said to the taxi driver, "My husband will be right back. He's just going upstairs to say goodbye to his mother."

A few minutes later, the husband climbed into the car and said, "I'm sorry I took so long. The old thing was hiding under the bed, so I had to poke her with a coat hanger to get her to come out!"

......................................

What do you call a lemon-eating cat?
  *Sourpuss.*

......................................

A persistent salesman was going door-to-door, and he knocked on the door of a woman who was not happy to see him. She told him in no uncertain terms that she did not want to hear his sales pitch and slammed the door in his face. To her surprise, however, the door did not close; in fact, it flew back open. She tried again, pushing on it as hard as she could, but met with the same result. The door bounced back open a second time.

Convinced that this pushy salesman was sticking his foot in the door, she reared back to give it a slam that would teach him a lesson, when he said, "Ma'am, before you do that again, I would suggest you move your cat."

..................................................

What do you call a cat that has been thrown in the dryer?

*Fluffy.*

# Cats, Wild

Why did the tiger eat the tightrope
walker?

*He wanted a well-balanced meal.*

...................................................

A police officer saw a woman sitting
in her car with a tiger in the front
seat next to her. The officer said, "It's
against the law to have that tiger in
your car. Take him to the zoo."

The next day the police officer
saw the same woman in the same car
with the same tiger. He said, "I told
you yesterday to take that tiger to
the zoo!"

The woman replied, "I did. He had such a good time, today we're going to the beach!"

......................................................

Why is it hard to spot a leopard in the jungle?
*Because they are born spotted.*

......................................................

A missionary was walking through the jungle one day. As he came into a clearing, he and a lion came face-to-face. In his shock, he dropped the rifle he had been carrying. He began to run as fast as he could and came upon a tree that he began to climb.

That was the good news. The bad news was the lion was charging at him, gaining speed and momentum.

"Dear Lord," the missionary prayed, "I really need Your help. Please, make that lion a Christian!"

Suddenly, the lion skidded to a halt, fell to its knees, clasped its paws together, and began to pray, "Dear God, please bless this food that I am about to receive. . . ."

"I came face-to-face with a lion once. And can you believe, I found myself alone and without a gun."

"What did you do?"

"What choice did I have? First, I tried looking straight into his eyes, but he slowly began to creep toward me. I moved back, but he kept coming. I had to do some quick thinking."

"So how did you get away?"

"I just left him and passed on to the next cage."

........................................

Mr. and Mrs. Phillips were on safari in darkest Africa. They were walking cautiously through the jungle when suddenly a huge lion leaped out in front of them, seized Mrs. Phillips in its jaws, and started to drag her away.

"Shoot!" she screamed to her husband. "Shoot!"

"I can't!" he yelled back. "The camera batteries are dead!"

What does the lion say to his friends before they go out hunting for food?
*"Let us prey."*

What is a lion's favorite food?
*Baked beings.*

What happened when the lion ate the comedian?
*He felt funny.*

How does a lion greet the other animals in the field?
*"Pleased to eat you."*

What's the difference between a tiger and a lion?
*A tiger has the mane part missing.*

What happened to the leopard that took a bath three times a day?
*After a week he was spotless.*

On which day do lions eat best?
*Chewsday.*

What happens when a lion runs into an express train at the station?

*It's the end of the lion.*

......................................................

How does a leopard change its spots?

*When it gets tired of one spot, it moves to another.*

......................................................

What do you call a lion that has eaten your mother's sister?

*An aunt-eater.*

......................................................

Which big cat should you never play a board game with?

*A cheetah.*

......................................................

Why aren't leopards any good at hide-and-seek?

*Because they're always spotted.*

# Chickens

Why was the chicken sent to the principal's office?

*Because it kept pecking on the other kids.*

......................................

Two hens were pecking around the chicken yard when suddenly a softball sailed over the fence and landed just inches from them.

One hen turned to the other and said, "Do you see that? Look at the eggs they're turning out next door!"

......................................

Why did the chewing gum cross the road?

*Because it was stuck to the chicken's foot.*

What has feathers and writes?

*A ballpoint hen.*

.......................................................

Larry had never cooked a day in his life but thought he'd like to surprise his wife with a special dinner on her birthday. He went out to the barn, selected a chicken, plucked it, and popped it into the oven.

An hour later he discovered he hadn't turned the oven on. As he opened the door, the chicken sat up and said, "Look, mister, can you either turn on the heat or give me back my feathers?"

.......................................................

Why was the chicken team so bad at baseball?

*They kept hitting fowl balls.*

.......................................................

One day a man was driving down a country road at about thirty miles per hour when he noticed a three-legged chicken running beside his car. He stepped on the accelerator, but at fifty miles per hour, the chicken was still keeping up. After about a mile, the chicken ran up a farm lane and into a barn behind an old farmhouse.

The man was so amazed that he turned around and drove up the farm lane. He knocked at the door and, when the farmer answered, told him what he had just seen.

The farmer said that he knew about the chicken. As a matter of fact, the farmer said that his son was a geneticist. He had developed this breed of chicken because the three of them each liked drumsticks, and this way they'd only have to kill one chicken for a meal.

The man said, "That's the most incredible story I have ever heard. So how do they taste?"

The farmer answered, "Don't know. We can't catch 'em."

........................................................

Why did Mozart sell his chickens?
*They kept saying, "Bach, Bach, Bach."*

The farmer's son was returning from the county fair with the crate of chickens his father had given him, when suddenly the box fell and broke open. Chickens flew everywhere, but the determined boy walked all over the field, gathering up the wayward birds and returning them to the repaired crate.

Hoping he had found them all, the boy reluctantly returned home, expecting the worst. "Pa, I'm sorry. The chickens got loose," the boy confessed sadly. "But I did manage to find all twelve of them."

"Well, you did real good then, Son," the farmer beamed. "You left here with eight."

...................................................

The customer wanted to buy a chicken and the butcher had only one in stock. He weighed it and said, "This one's a beauty. That will be $4.25."

"Oh, but that isn't quite large enough," said the customer. The butcher put the chicken back in the refrigerator, rolled it around on the ice several times, then placed it back on the scale again.

"This one is $5.50," he said, adding his thumb to the weight.

"Oh, that's great!" said the customer. "I'll take both of them, please."

......................................

Why did the chicken cross the road?
*To prove to the opossum that it could be done.*

......................................

Several scientists designed a gun specifically to launch dead chickens at the windshields of airplanes and military jets traveling at maximum velocity. The idea was to simulate the frequent incidents of collisions with airborne fowl to test the strength of the windshields.

Some engineers heard about the gun and were eager to test it on the windshields of high-speed trains.

Arrangements were made, and a gun was sent to the engineers. When the gun was fired, the engineers stood amazed as the chicken hurtled out of the barrel, crashed into the shatter-proof shield, smashed it into pieces, tore through the control panel, snapped the pilot's backrest in two, and embedded itself in the back wall of the cabin. The dismayed engineers sent the scientists the catastrophic results of the experiment, along with the designs for the windshield, and begged the scientists for suggestions.

The engineers soon received a one-line memo in response: "First, thaw the chicken."

....................................................

Which side of a chicken has the most feathers?

*The outside.*

....................................................

What do you get if you feed gunpowder to a chicken?

*An egg-splosion!*

A city man, tired of the rat race, decided to give up city life, move to the country, and become a chicken farmer. He purchased a nice, old chicken farm.

He soon discovered that his next-door neighbor was also a chicken farmer. The neighbor came to visit one day and offered, "Chicken farming isn't easy. To help you get started, I'd like to give you one hundred chickens."

The new chicken farmer was elated. Three weeks later the neighbor stopped by to see how things were going. The new farmer said, "Not very well. All one hundred chickens died."

The neighbor, astonished, said, "Oh, I can't believe that! I've never had any trouble with my chickens. I'll give you a hundred more."

Another three weeks went by, and the neighbor stopped in again. The new farmer said, "You won't believe it, but the second hundred chickens died too."

Astounded, the neighbor asked, "What did you do to them? What went wrong?"

"Well," said the new farmer, "I'm not quite sure. But I think maybe I'm not planting them far enough apart."

......................................

Two farmers meet on a dusty country road. One of them is carrying a big bag labeled "Chickens."

"Chickens, huh?" says one farmer. "How 'bout this. If I guess how many chickens you got, will you give me one of 'em?"

"Hey," says the guy with the bag, "if you guess right, I'll give you both of 'em."

The other scratches his head and guesses, "Um. . .four?"

......................................

Why did the Roman chicken cross the road?

*Because she was afraid someone would Caesar.*

What goes "peck, bang, peck, bang, peck, bang"?

*A bunch of chickens in a field full of balloons.*

..................................................

What kind of shoes do the chickens wear to cross the road?

*Ree-bok-bok-boks.*

# Cows

Why did the cows fail the test?
*They copied off each udder.*

......................................................

A city man named Smith was driving through the countryside when his car suddenly sputtered and coasted to a stop. *I have plenty of gas*, he thought, *so it must be the engine.*

He lifted the hood and tinkered with this and that but couldn't figure out the source of the problem.

"The trouble is with the carburetor," a deep voice behind him said. But when he turned, all he could see was a bull.

"Did, um, did you, uh, say something?" Smith asked.

"Yes," the bull replied. "I said the trouble is with the carburetor." Then he walked toward the car and peered under the hood.

Meanwhile, the man took off like a shot for a farmhouse down the road, where he told the farmer what had happened.

"Is this a big bull with a floppy right ear?" the farmer asked.

"Yes! That's the one!"

"Well, I wouldn't pay much attention to him if I were you," the farmer said. "That bull doesn't know as much about cars as he thinks he does."

......................................................

How did the farmer's wife keep track of their farm's steer population?
*She used cattle logs.*

......................................................

What do you call cattle with a sense of humor?
*Laughing stock.*

......................................................

What do you call a cow that eats grass?
*A lawn mooer.*

What do you call a calf after it's one year old?

*Two years old.*

......................................

What do you call a cow that has just given birth?

*Decalfinated.*

......................................

What do you call a sleeping bull?

*A bulldozer.*

......................................

What do you get from a pampered cow?

*Spoiled milk.*

......................................

What happened to the cow that survived an earthquake?

*She became a milk shake.*

......................................

City Slicker: "What's the name of this ranch?"

Rancher: "Why, it's the Double-D Crooked-T Bar-B Circle-M."

City Slicker: "It's kind of hard to remember all that, isn't it?"

Rancher: "I s'pose so."

City Slicker: "So where are all the cows?"

Rancher: "Can't keep any. One look at that branding iron, and they're gone!"

................................................

What is a cow's favorite form of entertainment?

*The moo-vies.*

................................................

Why do cows wear bells?

*Because their horns don't work.*

................................................

A stranger frantically ran up to a farmhouse door. He pounded his fist, and when the farmer came to the door the man demanded, "Where's the nearest railroad station, and what time is the next train into the city?"

The farmer thought for a moment. "Cut through my back hay-field, and you ought to reach the crossroads station in time for the 5:40. But if my bull spots you, I expect you'll make the 5:15."

What do you call a cow with a twitch?
*Beef jerky.*

...................................................

"Randy, name ten things with milk in them."

*"Coffee, cheese, ice cream, a milk shake, and, uh, six cows."*

...................................................

Two cows were visiting, chatting over the barbed wire fence that separated their farmers' fields.

"You know," the first bovine said, "this whole 'mad cow disease' thing is making me nervous. They say it spreads fast—and I've heard it's even struck some of the cows down on the Munson farm."

"Oh, I wouldn't worry about it," the second cow replied. "It won't affect us ducks."

...................................................

What did the lovesick bull say to the cow?

*"When I fall in love, it will be for heifer."*

What is cowhide most used for?
*Holding cows together.*

..................................................

What did the farmer call the cow that would not give him any milk?
*An udder failure.*

..................................................

A passenger train is creeping along very slowly. Finally it comes to a halt. A passenger sees a conductor walking by outside.

"Can you tell me what's going on?" she yells out the window.

"There's a cow on the tracks!" answers the conductor.

Ten minutes later, the train resumes its slow pace.

Within five minutes, however, it stops once again.

The woman sees the same conductor walking past the window again.

She leans out and yells, "What happened? Did we catch up with the cow again?"

What game do cows play at parties?
*Moo-sical chairs.*

......................................................

What are those spots on black-and-white cows?
*Hol-stains.*

# Deer

A reindeer walked into an ice cream shop, hopped up on a stool at the counter, and ordered a one-dollar hot butterscotch sundae.

When it arrived, he put a ten-dollar bill on the counter. But the waiter thought he wouldn't know anything about money and gave him only a dollar in change.

"You know," said the waiter, "we don't get many reindeer in here. In fact, I think you're the first one we've ever had."

"Well," the reindeer replied, "at nine dollars a sundae you probably won't get many more."

What do you give a deer with an upset stomach?

*Elk-a-seltzer.*

......................................................

It was early on a Saturday morning. Tom, an avid hunter, woke up ready to go bag the first deer of the season. He walked down to the kitchen to get some breakfast, and to his amazement he found his wife, Jill, sitting there, fully dressed in camouflage. Tom asked her, "What are you doing?"

Jill smiled and replied, "I want to go hunting with you!" Tom, though he had many reservations about it, reluctantly agreed that she could accompany him.

Later, they arrived at the hunting site. Tom sat his wife safely up in the tree stand and told her, "If you see a deer, aim carefully, and I'll come running back as soon as I hear the shot."

Tom walked away smiling, knowing that Jill couldn't bag an elephant, much less a deer. Not ten minutes had passed when he was startled by an array of gunshots.

Quickly, Tom started running back. As he got closer to her stand, he heard Jill screaming, "Get away from my deer!"

Bewildered, Tom raced faster toward his screaming wife. Again he heard her yell, "Get away from my deer!" followed by another volley of gunfire.

Within sight of where he had left his wife, Tom was surprised to see a man with his hands high in the air. The man, obviously distraught, said, "Okay, sure, ma'am. You can have your deer. Just let me get my saddle off it."

.......................................................

Two hunters were dragging a deer back to their truck when another hunter met up with them. "I sure don't mean to tell you what to do," he said, "but I think you'll find it much easier if you drag the deer the other way so the antlers don't dig into the ground."

After the hunter left, the two decided to try it his way. After a while, one said to the other, "That guy was right. This is a lot easier."

"Yeah," the other agreed, "but we keep getting further and further away from the truck."

# Dinosaurs

What do you call a blind dinosaur?
*Do-you-think-he-saurus.*

..................................................

What do you call a sleeping dinosaur?
*A bronto-snore-us.*

..................................................

What do you call a dinosaur that
steps on everything in its way?
*Tyrannosaurus wrecks.*

..................................................

Why do dinosaurs have wrinkles in
their knees?
*They stayed in the swimming pool
too long.*

# Dogs

"Why is your dog growling at me while I'm eating?" Dave asked Steve. "Does he want me to give him some food?"

"No," said Steve. "He's just mad because you're eating off his favorite plate."

What animal says, "Baa-baa-woof"?
*A sheepdog.*

In a small town the veterinarian, who was also the chief of police, was awakened by the telephone.

"Please hurry!" said the woman's voice on the other end of the line.

"Do you need the police or a vet?" he asked.

"Both," the woman replied. "I'm not able to get my dog's mouth open, and there's a burglar's leg in it."

......................................

For several years the man trained his dog to tell jokes and sing songs. One day he got the dog his first break, a spot on a TV talk show. When the dog came onstage, however, he froze and didn't say a word.

On the way home, the man was impatient and angry with the dog. "We had a shot at stardom, and you blew it. What in the world happened?"

"I couldn't see the cue cards," complained the dog.

......................................

A woman frantically dialed 911. "You've got to help me," she said. "I've lost my dog!"

"Sorry, ma'am," said the dispatcher, "but we don't handle missing animals."

"You don't understand. This is no ordinary dog. He can talk."

"Well, you better hang up. He might be trying to call in."

......................................................

Little Henry got a violin and played it night and day. Unfortunately, every time he played a note, the family dog would whine and howl endlessly.

One afternoon, unable to stand the dog's suffering any longer, Henry's little sister stormed into his room and begged, "For goodness' sake! Can't you please play something the dog doesn't know?"

......................................................

How do you make a puppy disappear?

*Use Spot remover.*

......................................................

A man walks into a diner carrying a dog in his arms. He places the dog on the counter and proclaims that the dog can talk. The man says he has one hundred dollars he's willing to bet anyone who says he can't. The waiter quickly takes the bet, and the dog's owner looks at the dog and asks him, "What's the thing on top of a building that keeps the sun and rain out?"

The dog answers, "Roof."

The waiter says, "Are you kidding? I'm not paying."

The dog's owner says, "Double or nothing, and I'll ask him a different question." The waiter agrees, and the owner turns to his dog and asks, "Who was the greatest baseball player ever?"

The dog answers with a muffled, "Ruth."

With that the waiter picks them both up and throws them out on the street. As they bounce on the sidewalk in front of the diner, the dog looks at his owner and says, "DiMaggio?"

What do you get when you cross Lassie with a petunia?

*A collie flower.*

......................................................

Why did the Doberman marry the golden retriever?

*He found her very fetching.*

......................................................

What do you call a pooch that wakes up too early in the morning?

*A groggy doggy.*

......................................................

Man: "Are you certain this dog you're selling me is loyal?"

Owner: "Of course he is. I sold him five times, and every time he's come back."

......................................................

A local business was looking for office help. The owners put a sign in the window that read HELP WANTED. MUST BE ABLE TO TYPE, MUST BE GOOD WITH A COMPUTER, AND MUST BE BILINGUAL. WE ARE AN EQUAL OPPORTUNITY EMPLOYER.

A short time later, a dog walked up to the window, saw the sign, and went inside. He looked at the receptionist and wagged his tail, then walked over to the sign, looked at it, and barked. The receptionist got the idea and told the office manager. The office manager looked at the dog and was surprised, to say the least. However, the dog looked determined, so the manager took him into his office. Inside, the dog took a seat on one of the chairs and stared at the manager. The manager said, "I can't hire you. The sign says you have to be able to type." The dog jumped down, went to the typewriter, and typed out a perfect letter. He took out the page and handed it to the manager, then jumped back on the chair. The manager was amazed but then told the dog, "The sign says you have to be good with a computer." The dog went to the computer and entered a program that ran perfectly the first time.

By now, the manager was totally dumbfounded. He looked at the dog and said, "I realize that you are quite an intelligent dog and have some very interesting skills. However, I still can't give you the job." The dog jumped down, went to a copy of the sign, and put his paw on the sentence that read WE ARE AN EQUAL OPPORTUNITY EMPLOYER.

The manager said, "Yes, but the sign also says that you must speak two languages."

The dog looked at the manager and said, "Meow."

..................................................

What do you call a dog with a cold?
*Germy shepherd.*

..................................................

One day, a busy butcher notices a dog in his shop and shoos it away. Later, he discovers the dog has returned and is carrying a note in its mouth. The note says, "Can I have twelve sausages and a leg of lamb, please?" The butcher looks, and sure enough, there is a ten-dollar bill in the dog's mouth. So the man retrieves the money, places the sausages and lamb in a bag, and puts the bag in the dog's mouth. Since it's about closing time, the butcher decides to close up shop and see where the dog goes.

The animal walks down the street to a crosswalk. It puts down the bag, jumps up, and presses the crossing button. Then it picks up the bag and waits patiently for the light to change.

Soon, the dog walks across the road with the butcher following close behind. At a bus stop, the animal examines the timetable. The dog checks out the bus times, then finds a place on one of the seats to wait. The butcher is amazed.

When a bus rolls up, the dog gets up, looks at the number, and returns to his seat. Another bus pulls in shortly, and the dog, making sure it's the right bus, climbs on. The butcher, by now completely shocked, follows the dog onto the bus, which travels through town and out to the suburbs. After several miles, the dog gets up and moves to the front. Standing on its hind legs, he rings the bell to stop the bus. The dog gets off with the bag still in its mouth. The butcher continues to follow close behind.

They walk down the road, and the dog turns toward a house, walking up the path and dropping the bag on the step. Then it backtracks down the path, takes a big run, and throws itself—whap!—against the door. No one comes to the door, so the dog repeats its run and jump against the door. There is still no response from inside the home.

The dog goes back down the path, leaps up onto a narrow wall, and walks along the perimeter of the garden. It reaches a window and bangs its head against the glass several times. Then it walks back, jumps off the wall, and waits at the door. Finally, a big guy opens the door and starts yelling at the dog.

The butcher runs up and scolds the angry man. "What are you doing?" he says. "This dog is a genius. It could be on TV!"

"Genius?" the other man says. "This is the second time this week he's forgotten his key!"

......................................

What composer is the favorite among dogs?
*Poochini.*

......................................

Where do little dogs sleep when they go camping?
*In pup tents.*

......................................

There was a knight who was very brave but a little odd. While all the other knights rode horses, he preferred to ride his faithful Great Dane.

One night, returning from a trip, the knight was caught in a downpour and sought shelter at an inn. The innkeeper did not like knights and refused to give him a room. But when he saw the dog standing there soaking wet, his heart softened.

"I couldn't turn a knight out on a dog like this," he said.

......................................................

A salesman dropped in to see a business customer. No one was in the office. However, he did find a big dog emptying wastebaskets. The salesman stared at the animal, wondering if his imagination could be playing tricks on him.

The dog looked up and said, "Don't be surprised. This is just part of my job."

"Incredible!" exclaimed the man. "I can't believe it. Does your boss know how incredible you are? An animal that can talk!"

"Oh no," pleaded the dog. "Please

don't say anything! If he finds out I can talk, he'll make me answer the phone too."

......................................

Where do you take a sick puppy?
*To the dog-tor.*

......................................

Where do dogs like to go river rafting?
*In Collie-rado.*

......................................

The ad in the local newspaper read: "Purebred Police Dog $25.00." Thinking that to be an exceptional bargain, Mrs. Rogers ordered the dog to be delivered.

The next day a van pulled up and left her the scruffiest, mangiest-looking mongrel she had ever seen. In a rage, she telephoned the man who had placed the ad. "How can you call that mangy mutt a purebred police dog?"

"Don't be deceived by his looks, ma'am," the man replied. "He's with the Secret Service."

What happened to the puppy that ate an onion?

*His bark was much worse than his bite.*

................................................

What do you call a poodle in a sauna?

*A hot dog.*

................................................

Four men were boasting of the merits of their favorite four-legged friend.

"My ol' Penny goes to the store for me," said one. "She always brings me back my evening newspaper."

"My dog Lacey buys our grits at that same store," said another. "I give her a ten-dollar bill, and she brings me back the change first, then returns for the bag of grits."

"I send ol' Pogo there for my shotgun shells," said the third. "He knows exactly what gauge and brand I want."

The fourth man said nothing until he was challenged by the others to try to top their tales.

"I reckon my dog ain't much to speak of, by comparison," he answered. "He just sits in the store all day and runs the cash register."

...................................................

What bone will a dog never eat?
*A trombone.*

...................................................

What would you get if you crossed a hunting dog and a telephone?
*A golden receiver.*

...................................................

When does a man act like a dog?
*When he's a boxer.*

...................................................

How does a dog turn off the DVD player?
*He presses the PAWS button.*

...................................................

A man telephoned his neighbor at four o'clock in the morning and said, "Your dog is barking and keeping me awake."

The neighbor called him back at

4:00 a.m. the next day and said, "I don't have a dog."

.................................................

A mother, much against her better judgment, finally gave in and bought the children a dog with the understanding that they would care for it. They named the dog Laddy. It wasn't long before the responsibility fell to the mother, and she found that she was taking care of the dog all by herself. Since the children did not live up to their promise, she decided to sell Laddy.

One of them sorrowfully said, "We'll miss him."

Another said, "If he wouldn't eat so much and wouldn't be so messy, could we please keep him?"

Mom stood strong and held her ground. "It's time to take Laddy to his new home."

"Laddy?" the children asked. "We thought you said *Daddy*."

What kind of trees do puppies like best?

*Dogwood. They like its bark.*

......................................................

A little boy bought a box of soap flakes, telling the clerk he needed to wash his dog. The clerk told him to be very careful because it was a strong detergent.

The next time the boy came in, the clerk asked him about his dog, and the boy said, "He died."

"Well, I told you that I thought it would be too strong to wash a little dog," the clerk said.

"I don't think it was that," the boy explained. "I think it was the rinse cycle that got him."

......................................................

Upon entering a little country store, a stranger noticed a sign reading: Danger! Beware of Dog, posted on the glass door.

Inside, he noticed a harmless old hound dog asleep on the floor beside the counter. He asked the store manager, "Is that the dog folks are supposed to beware of?"

"Yup, sure is," he replied.

The stranger couldn't help but smile in amusement. "That certainly doesn't appear to be a dangerous dog to me. Why did you post that sign?"

"Well," the owner replied, "before I posted that sign, people kept tripping over him."

......................................................

A man walked into the office of a psychiatrist and sat down to explain his problem. "Doctor, I have this problem," the man said. "I keep hallucinating that I'm a dog. It's crazy. I don't know what to do!"

"A common canine complex," said the doctor reassuringly. "Relax. Come here and lie down on the couch."

"Oh, I can't, Doctor," the man said nervously. "I'm not allowed up on the furniture."

What goes tick-tick woof-woof?
  *A watchdog.*

..................................................

A woman was out looking for a pet. She walked into a small pet shop and explained her interest to the owner. He thought for a moment and said, "I think I have just the thing for you, ma'am. I'll just get him."

He disappeared into a back room and returned with a cute little puppy. "This dog is a very special dog," he told her. "It can fly." Then he threw the dog into the air. It immediately began to float gracefully around the shop.

"There is one problem with him, however," the shop owner said. "Whenever you say 'my,' he will eat whatever you've mentioned. Look: 'My cookie!' " The lady watched in amazement as the dog zoomed over to the man and devoured a cookie he'd taken from his pocket.

"He's extraordinary—and cute!" the woman gushed. "I'll take him." A few minutes later she was walking the dog home to show her husband.

Opening the front door, she called out, "Sweetheart, look at this amazing pet I bought today. . .he can fly!"

The husband looked at the dog with a frown and said, "Fly? Ha! My foot!"

....................................................

What wears a coat all winter and pants in the summer?

*A dog.*

....................................................

One afternoon, a woman was hanging laundry in the backyard when an old, tired-looking dog wandered onto her property. She could tell from his collar and well-fed stomach that he had an owner. But when she walked into the house, he followed her, sauntered down the hall, and fell asleep in a corner. Almost an hour later, he went to the door, and she let him out.

The next day the dog was back.

He resumed his position in the hallway and slept for an hour. This continued for a couple of weeks. Curious, the woman pinned a note to his collar: "Every afternoon your dog has been coming to my house and taking a nap."

The next day the dog arrived with a different note pinned to his collar: "Duke lives in a home with six children—he's trying to catch up on his sleep."

......................................................

Where does a dog go when he loses his tail?

*To the re-tailer.*

......................................................

Why did the poor dog chase his own tail?

*He was trying to make both ends meet.*

......................................................

A city man was vacationing at a ranch. The farmer he was staying with said, "It's a beautiful morning.

Why don't you take the dogs and do a bit of shooting?"

"Great!" said the man. "Thanks!"

At lunch the farmer inquired, "How was the shooting?"

"Terrific. Got any more dogs?"

..................................................

What did the hungry dalmatian say when he had a meal?

*"That hit the spots."*

..................................................

What dog can jump higher than a tree?

*Any dog can jump higher than a tree. Trees don't jump.*

..................................................

A very intelligent boy was fortunate enough to receive more education than his parents had, and his vocabulary far outmatched theirs. One day he came home from school and said, "Mother, may I relate to you a narrative?"

"What's a narrative, Harold?" she asked.

"A narrative, Mother, is a tale."

"Oh, I see," said his mother nodding, and Harold told her the story. At bedtime as he was about to go upstairs, he said, "Shall I extinguish the light, Mother?"

"What's extinguish?" she asked.

"Extinguish means to put out, Mother," said Harold.

"Oh, okay. Yes, certainly."

The next day the pastor stopped in for a visit, and the family dog began to make a nuisance of himself, as dogs will, by begging for goodies from the table. "Harold," said his mother, trying to impress, "please take that dog by the narrative and extinguish him!"

..................................................

What should you do if you find a five-hundred-pound dog asleep on your bed?

*Sleep on the sofa.*

What should you do if you find a five-hundred-pound dog wearing your favorite tie?

*Go see a doctor. You have been seeing too many five-hundred-pound dogs lately.*

..................................................

What do you call a litter of young dogs that have come in from the snow?

*Slush puppies.*

..................................................

How do you find your dog if he's lost in the woods?

*Put your ear up to a tree and listen for the bark.*

..................................................

What did the dog get when he multiplied 413 by 782?

*The wrong answer.*

..................................................

A notice in a weekly newspaper advertised bulldog puppies: "Cute, already housebroken," the advertiser promised. "Eat most any food you put in front of them. Love children."

# Elephants

What is big and gray and weighs down the front of your car?

*An elephant in the glove compartment.*

How can you tell how old an elephant is?

*Count the candles on its birthday cake.*

Why do elephants paint their toenails red?

*So they can hide in the strawberry patch.*

What time is it when an elephant sits on the fence?

*Time to fix the fence.*

..................................................

Jeweler: "Hello, 911. I own a jewelry store and an elephant just walked in, sucked up all the jewelry with his trunk, and ran out."

Police: "Can you give me a description?"

Jeweler: "Not really, because he was wearing a mask."

..................................................

What do you give a seasick elephant?

*Lots of space.*

..................................................

What do you call an elephant in a Honda?

*Stuck.*

..................................................

Why was the vacationing elephant so glum?

*The airline lost his trunk.*

..................................................

What do you call an elephant on the run?

*An earthquake.*

A hungry man saw a sign in a restaurant window saying We'll Pay $100.00 to Anyone Who Orders Something We Can't Make.

When he was seated at his table, he said to the waitress, "I'll have an elephant sandwich."

Reaching into her apron, the waitress pulled out a roll of bills and handed the man one hundred dollars.

"What?" said the man as he pocketed the money. "No elephants today?"

"Oh, we have elephants, all right," sighed the waitress. "But we're all out of the big buns."

..................................................

Why did the elephant leave the circus?
*He was tired of working for peanuts.*

..................................................

How do you make an elephant laugh?
*Tickle him.*

What do you get when you cross an elephant and a jar of peanut butter?
*Either an elephant that sticks to the roof of your mouth, or a jar of peanut butter with a long memory.*

......................................................

Why do elephants have trunks?
*Because they don't have hoods.*

......................................................

How does an elephant climb a tree?
*It sits on an acorn and waits.*

......................................................

How does an elephant come down out of a tree?
*He stands on a leaf and waits for autumn.*

......................................................

Two elephants were discussing life in general.

"You know," stated one, "we're considered by human scientists to possess the best memories of any animals on the face of the globe."

"Well then," said the other, "why can't I remember where I left my bag of peanuts?"

Why is an elephant large, gray, hairy, and wrinkled?

> *Because if he were small, white, hairless, and smooth, he'd be an aspirin.*

.................................................

What would you do if an elephant sat in front of you at the movies?

> *Miss most of the movie.*

.................................................

Everyone knows that an elephant never forgets—but then, what does he really have to remember?

.................................................

What vegetable do you get when an elephant walks through your garden?

> *Squash.*

# Fish

A fisherman's wife had twin sons. The parents were thrilled but couldn't think of what to name them. Finally, after a few days, the fisherman said, "Let's not decide on names right now. If we wait a little while, I'm certain the names will simply come to us."

After several weeks had passed, the fisherman and his wife noticed something strange. When left alone, one of the boys would always turn toward the sea, while the other boy would face inland. It didn't matter which way the parents positioned the lads, the same child always faced the same direction. "Let's call the boys Toward and Away," suggested the fisherman. His wife agreed, and from that point on, the boys were known simply as Toward and Away.

The years passed, and the sons grew tall and strong. The day came when the fisherman said to them, "Boys, it is time that you learn how to make a living from the sea." The three of them filled their ship with supplies, said their farewells, and set sail for a three-day voyage. At the end of the third day, the ship had not returned. Another three days passed, and still no ship. Three weeks passed before the woman saw a lone man walking toward her house. She knew it was her husband. "My goodness!" she cried. "What has happened to my darling boys?"

The ragged fisherman began to tell his story: "We were just barely one whole day out to sea when Toward hooked into a great fish. Toward fought long and hard, but the fish was more than his equal. For a whole week they wrestled upon the waves without either of them letting up. Yet eventually the great fish started to win the battle, and Toward was pulled over the side of our ship. He was swallowed whole, and we never saw either of them again."

"Oh, how terrible!" said the fisherman's wife. "What a huge fish that must have been!"

"Yes, it was," the man replied, sobbing. "But you should have seen the one that got Away!"

...................................................

Why don't fish like to go online?
*Because they're afraid of getting caught in the net.*

...................................................

What do you call a fish with no eye?
*A fsh.*

...................................................

Why are fish so smart?
*Because they live in schools.*

Guide: "I never guide hunters any-more, just fishermen."

Hunter: "Why?"

Guide: "I've never been mistaken for fish."

.....................................................

A game warden noticed how a man named Herb consistently caught more fish than anyone else. While the other guys would only catch three or four fish a day, Herb would come in off the lake with a boatful. Stringer after stringer was always packed with freshly caught trout. The warden, curious, asked Herb his secret.

The successful fisherman invited the game warden to accompany him to observe. So the next morning the two met at the dock and set out in Herb's boat. When they got to the middle of the lake, Herb stopped the boat, and the warden sat back to see how it was done.

Herb's approach was quite simple.

He took a stick of dynamite, lit it, and threw it in the air. The explosion rocked the lake with such a force that dead fish immediately rose to the surface. Herb took out a net and started scooping them up.

When the game warden recovered from his shock, he began yelling at Herb. "You can't do this! I'll put you in jail, buddy! You will be paying every fine there is in the book!"

Meanwhile, Herb put the net down and took out another stick of dynamite. He lit it and tossed it in the lap of the game warden. "Well, Warden, are you going to sit there all day complaining, or are you going to fish?"

......................................................

Two men went on a fishing trip. They rented all the equipment: the reels, the rods, the wading suits, the rowboat, the car, and even a cabin in the woods. They spent a fortune.

The first day they went fishing,

but they didn't catch a thing. The same thing happened on the second day, as well as on the third day. It went on like that until finally, on the last day of their vacation, one of the men caught a fish.

On the drive home, the men were really depressed. One guy turned to the other and said, "Do you realize that this one lousy fish we caught cost us fifteen-hundred bucks?"

"Wow!" said his buddy. "It's a good thing we didn't catch any more."

What's the difference between a fish and a piano?

*You can't tuna fish.*

One afternoon, a twelve-year-old boy was taking care of his baby sister while his parents went to town to go shopping. The boy decided to go fishing, but he had to take his baby sister along.

"I will never do that again," the boy told his mother later that evening. "I couldn't catch a thing! I didn't even get a bite."

"Oh, next time I'm sure your sister will be quiet and not scare the fish away," his mother said.

"That's not it," the boy grumbled. "She ate all the bait."

..................................................

Where do fish wash?
*In a river basin.*

..................................................

Two serious anglers went fishing in a rowboat. For four hours neither of them moved a muscle. Then the one up forward became a bit restless.

"Will you stop that?" grumbled his companion. "That's the second time you've shifted your feet in twenty minutes. Did you come out here to fish or dance?"

..................................................

What game do fish like playing the most?
*Name that tuna.*

What kind of money do fishermen make?

*Net profits.*

# Frogs

A frog expert from the aquarium visited a third-grade class to give a talk on amphibians.

"It's easy to tell the male frogs from the female frogs," said the man, as he held up two cages. "When you feed them, the male frog will eat only female flies, and the female frogs will eat only male flies."

One boy in the back of the room raised his hand. "But how do you tell which flies are male and which are female?"

"How would I know?" replied the man. "I'm a frog expert."

Two frogs were sitting on a log, feeding on passing insects. One remarked to the other, "Time's sure fun when we're having flies."

...................................................

What's white on the outside, green on the inside, and hops?

*A frog sandwich.*

...................................................

What happens when a frog's car breaks down?

*He gets toad away.*

...................................................

What did the croaking frog say to his friend?

*"Excuse me, I think I've got a person in my throat."*

...................................................

Where do tadpoles change into frogs?

*In the croakroom.*

...................................................

What would you get if you crossed a baseball player with a frog?

*An outfielder who catches flies— and then eats them.*

# Goats

Two guys were walking through the woods and came across a big hole. "Wow, that looks deep," one said.

"It sure does!" the other replied.

"Toss a few pebbles in there and see how deep it is." They picked up stones, threw them in, and waited, but heard no noise.

"Man, that is really deep," the first guy said. "Here, throw one of those big rocks down there. That should make a noise." So they picked up a couple of football-sized rocks, tossing them into the hole. They waited and waited but again heard nothing.

The guys looked at each other in amazement. One shook his head— and caught a glimpse of something in the underbrush. "Look, over here in the weeds—it's a railroad tie. Help me carry it over to the hole. When we toss that in, it'll have to make a noise!"

So the two dragged the heavy tie over to the hole and threw it in. There was still not a sound from the hole.

But suddenly, out of the woods, a goat appeared, running like the wind. It charged forward and right past the men, running as fast as its legs would carry it. All of a sudden, it leaped into the air and shot down into the hole.

The two guys were standing stunned, when a man appeared in the woods. An old farmer spotted the men and ambled over to them. "Howdy!" he said. "You two guys seen my goat out here anywhere?"

"We sure did!" they answered. "Craziest thing we've ever seen. It came running like the wind and just jumped into this hole!"

"Nah," said the farmer, "that couldn't have been my goat. He was chained up to a railroad tie."

......................................................

Why can't goats eat round bales of hay?

*Because they need three square meals a day.*

......................................................

What do you call a goat's beard?

*A goatee.*

......................................................

What animal makes it hard to carry on a conversation?

*A goat—he always wants to butt in.*

# Horses

One September, a group of third-graders were surprised to discover their new teacher was a stallion. He was a big, strong horse, but he had a high-pitched voice. The class thought this was hysterical, and the children laughed every time he opened his mouth. The poor animal spent whole days yelling and screaming for order.

Finally, the stallion lost his voice one day. He stepped out of the schoolhouse for a while, and the children saw him walking toward a nearby farm. Before long, he returned with a pony.

This horse was small, but he had a deep voice. Soon, he was bellowing, "You kids pay attention or else!" The kids got back in their seats and quieted down.

It just goes to show you: to get things done, sometimes you have to shout until you get a little horse.

........................................

Why did the pony get sent to the principal's office?

*It was horsing around.*

........................................

How many legs does a horse have?

*Six. It has forelegs in the front and two legs in the back.*

........................................

The door to the Pony Express office swung open, and a cowboy sprinted outside. He took a running jump and landed on his bottom in the middle of the street.

"What's the matter with you,

pardner?" asked a bystander. "Did you get thrown out, or are you just plain crazy?"

"Neither," answered the cowboy. "But I'm gonna find the guy who moved my horse!"

..................................................

An out-of-towner drove his car into a country ditch. Fortunately, a local farmer came to help with his big, strong horse named Buddy. The man hitched Buddy up to the car and yelled, "Pull, Nellie, pull!" Buddy didn't move.

Then the farmer hollered, "Pull, Buster, pull!" Buddy didn't respond.

Once more the farmer commanded, "Pull, Jennie, pull!" Nothing happened.

Then the farmer nonchalantly said, "Pull, Buddy, pull." The horse easily dragged the car out of the ditch.

The motorist was grateful and curious, asking the farmer why he called his horse by the wrong name three times. The farmer replied, "Oh, Buddy is blind—if he thought he was the only one pulling, he wouldn't even try!"

........................................

Farmer Brown had been injured in an accident. Now he was in court, hoping to gain compensation.

The insurance company's lawyer asked the farmer, "Didn't you say at the scene of the accident, 'I'm fine'?"

Farmer Brown responded, "Well, I can tell you what happened: I had just loaded my favorite horse, Sally, into the—"

"I didn't ask for details," the lawyer interrupted. "Just answer the question: Did you not say, at the scene of the accident, 'I'm fine'?"

Farmer Brown said, "Well, I had just gotten Sally into the trailer, and I was driving down the road—"

The lawyer interrupted again, saying, "Judge, I am trying to establish the fact that, at the scene of the accident, this man told the officer that he was fine. Now, several weeks after the accident, he is trying to collect insurance money. I believe he is a fraud. Please tell him to simply answer the question."

The judge, though, was curious about the answer Farmer Brown was trying to give. "I'd like to hear what he has to say about Sally," the judge said.

Farmer Brown thanked the judge and proceeded. "Well, as I was saying, I had just loaded Sally, my favorite horse, into the trailer and was driving her down the highway when a huge semitruck ran the stop sign and smacked my truck right in the side.

"I was thrown into one ditch, and Sally was thrown into the other," he continued. "I was hurting real bad and didn't want to move. But I could hear ol' Sally moaning and groaning. I knew she was in terrible shape just by her groans.

"Soon, a police officer came on

the scene. He could hear Sally moaning and groaning, so he went over to her. After he looked at her, he took out his gun and shot her between the eyes. Then the officer came across the road with his gun in his hand and looked at me.

"The officer looked at me and said, 'Your horse was in such bad shape I had to shoot her. How are you feeling?' "

.......................................................

A husband and wife were driving down a country lane on their way to visit friends. They came to a muddy spot, and the car became stuck. After trying unsuccessfully to remove the car themselves, they noticed a farmer coming down the road, driving some horses before him. The man stopped and offered to pull the car out of the mud for fifty dollars. The husband agreed, and moments later the car was free.

Unhitching the tow rope, the farmer said, "You know, you're the tenth car I've helped out of the mud today."

The husband was surprised and asked the farmer, "When do you have time to plow your land? At night?"

"Oh no," the farmer replied. "Night is when I put the water in the hole."

......................................

What is the best type of story to tell a runaway horse?

*A tale of whoa.*

......................................

What did one horse say to the other horse?

*"The pace is familiar, but I can't remember the mane."*

......................................

A man rode into town on Monday, stayed for five days, and rode out on Monday. How is this possible?

*His horse's name was Monday.*

What has four legs and flies?
  *A horse in the summertime.*

..................................................

It was a beautiful afternoon when Tim said to George, "Hey, George, why don't we get ourselves a couple of horses? We could ride them in the summer, and in the winter we could put them in the paddock behind the house."

George thought that was a great idea, so the following day he and Tim went out and bought themselves two horses. They rode them in the summer, but when winter came George got worried. "Hey, Tim," he said, "how will we tell them apart next spring?"

Tim said, "Well, how 'bout I shave the mane off mine and you shave the tail off yours." This satisfied George, so they did.

The next spring when they returned to get the horses, they found their hair had all grown back. Alarmed, George said, "Oh great, now how are we going to tell them apart?"

Tim replied, "Well, why don't you take the black one, and I'll take the brown one."

...............................................

Two friends were watching a western. In the movie, the sheriff rode into a town where the bad guys were lying in wait. One friend said to the other, "I bet you ten dollars he falls off his horse."

"Don't be ridiculous," his buddy replied. "The good guy never falls off his horse."

"I bet he does."

"All right," said the second, "I'll bet you ten dollars he doesn't."

They sat in silence watching the film for a few more minutes; the bad guys began shooting. The sheriff's horse reared up—and the sheriff fell down!

"See, I told you so," said the first man.

"Oh, okay," said the second. "Here's your ten dollars."

"No, I can't take that," his friend said, shaking his head. "I have to admit—I've seen this movie before."

"So have I," the other man replied. "But I didn't think the sheriff would fall off again!"

......................................

A preacher was trying to sell his horse. A potential buyer came to the church for a test ride.

"Before you begin," the preacher said, "you need to know there is something special about this horse. You have to say, 'Praise the Lord,' to make it go and 'Amen' to make it stop."

So the man mounted the horse and said, "Praise the Lord," and the horse started to trot. The man again said, "Praise the Lord," and the horse started to gallop. Soon he saw a cliff ahead. In his fright, he yelled, "Whoa, stop!" The horse kept running. "Hey!"

he shouted. "Slow down!" But the horse charged on.

Then he remembered the term the horse understood: "Amen!" he cried.

The horse stopped just inches from the edge of the cliff. The man leaned back in the saddle, wiped the sweat from his brow, and said, "Whew, praise the Lord!"

# Kangaroos

Why does a mother kangaroo hope it doesn't rain?

*She doesn't like it when her children have to play inside.*

......................................

Why won't banks allow kangaroos to open accounts?

*Their checks always bounce.*

......................................

Why did the kangaroo lose the basketball game?

*He ran out of bounds.*

What's tan on the inside and red and gold on the outside?

*Campbell's Cream of Kangaroo soup.*

# Mice

What is a mouse's favorite sport?
  *Mice hockey.*

...............................................

What is gray and has four legs and a trunk?
  *A mouse going on vacation.*

...............................................

Hickory dickory dock,
The mice ran up the clock.
The clock struck one,
And the rest got away with minor
  injuries.

...............................................

What do you call a group of mice in disguise?
  *A mouse-querade party.*

How do you save a drowning mouse?
    *Use mouse-to-mouse resuscitation.*

..................................................

What have twelve legs, six eyes,
three tails, and cannot see?
    *Three blind mice.*

..................................................

Why did the mouse eat a candle?
    *For some light refreshment.*

# Monkeys

An astronaut graduated near the bottom of his class. On his first mission into space, he was teamed with an orangutan. The astronaut and the orangutan were each given an envelope that they were to open once they were in space.

Moments after blastoff, the orangutan opened his envelope, read the contents, and then began flicking buttons and hitting switches.

Eagerly opening his envelope, the astronaut was surprised to discover three words of instruction: "Feed the orangutan."

The country club pro was quite ego-tistical—good at the game and more than happy to remind anyone he defeated. When one of the members had his fill of the pro's attitude, he bought a gorilla and trained it to play golf. He then organized a game between the pro and the gorilla, with the loser to cough up one thousand dollars.

On the day of the match, the pro teed off on the first hole, a 525-yard par-5. He split the fairway some 270 yards out.

The gorilla then lumbered up to the tee. He swung with force, and everyone watching stood in awe as the ball disappeared into the sky. By the time it landed, it was only six inches from the cup.

The pro knew he was in trouble. If this were any indication of the way things would go, he would never live it down. He paid his opponent, saying he had just remembered some urgent business across town.

As the group walked from the tee, the pro asked, "So, how does he putt?"

The gorilla's manager replied with a smile, "The same way he drives—525 yards."

......................................

What would you get if you crossed a blimp with an orangutan?

*A hot-air baboon.*

......................................

How do you fix a broken chimp?

*With a monkey wrench.*

......................................

There was a man who owned a giant gorilla and, all its life, he had never left it on its own. But there came a time that he needed to go on a business trip and had to leave his gorilla in his next-door neighbor's care. He explained to his neighbor that all he had to do was feed his gorilla three bananas a day at three, six, and nine o'clock. But he was never, ever, ever to touch its fur.

The following day the man came and gave the gorilla a banana and studied it, thinking, *Why can't I touch its fur?* There didn't seem to be any harm in it. Every day the man looked for a little while longer, never understanding why he couldn't touch the animal's fur.

About a week later, he was so curious that he decided he *was* going to touch the gorilla. He passed it the banana and very gently brushed the back of his hand against its fur.

The gorilla went wild. It jumped up and down, and then began running toward the man. Terrified, the man turned and dashed through the front door, over the lawn, down the street, and into his car, driving off at high speed. In the rearview mirror, he could see the gorilla keeping pace, lumbering right behind him.

The man drove until the car's engine began to sputter and stopped.

So he jumped out and ran farther down the street, climbed over a brick wall into someone's front garden, and hauled himself up an apple tree. He looked back to find the gorilla right behind him, beating its chest.

The man, now screaming, jumped down and ran back into the street. He turned into a narrow alley, thinking he'd lost the beast when, suddenly, a giant shadow appeared on the street ahead. The gorilla!

The animal lumbered down the alley, directly toward the man, who was now paralyzed with fear. Its dark eyes burning, its powerful teeth bared, the gorilla raised its mighty hand over the man's head. Then it tapped his ear and said, "Tag! You're it!"

# Octopuses

How does an octopus go into battle?
*Fully armed.*

.................................................

First Octopus: "What do you hate
most about being an octopus?"
Second Octopus: "Washing my
hands before dinner."

.................................................

What does an octopus wear when it's
cold?
*A coat of arms.*

What did the boy octopus say to the girl octopus?

*"May I hold your hand, hand, hand, hand, hand, hand, hand, hand?"*

# Pigs

What did the pig say when he fell
down the stairs?
*"Oh, my achin' bacon."*

How did they catch the crooks at the
pig farm?
*Someone squealed.*

What is a pig's favorite ballet?
*Swine Lake.*

What do you get when you cross a
pig and a tree?
*A porky pine.*

What is a pig's favorite play?
   *Hamlet.*

..................................................

What do you call a pig doing karate?
   *A pork chop.*

..................................................

Do lady pigs join the sowing circle?
   *No, they're too busy bacon pies.*

..................................................

What do you give a pig with
a sore nose?
   *Oink-ment.*

..................................................

What happens if pigs fly?
   *Bacon goes up.*

..................................................

A pig went to the bank for a loan to
buy some trinkets for his new house.

"Hi, my name is Mr. Paddywhack,"
one of the bankers said. "How can I
help you?"

When the pig explained, the banker
frowned and said, "I'm sorry, but we
never lend money to animals."

"Please," requested the pig. "I

promise I'll pay it back."

"Perhaps you had better speak to the manager," insisted Mr. Paddywhack.

A few minutes later, the manager appeared, and the pig again pleaded, "Please, all I need is a little money to buy some trinkets."

"I told him we don't lend money to livestock," the banker retorted.

"Oh, for goodness' sake!" exclaimed the manager, throwing his hands up in the air. "It's a knickknack, Paddywhack—give the hog a loan!"

..................................................

A farmer was bragging to his friends about his pig. "That animal saved my life twice," he said. "Once I fell into the river, and he jumped in and dragged me to the bank. Another time my house caught on fire, and he went in and saved me, my wife, and kids." The farmer passed around a picture of the miraculous animal. One of the guys noticed the pig was missing a leg.

"Which accident did the pig lose its leg in?" he asked.

"Neither," the farmer replied. "An animal like that you don't eat all at once!"

........................................

Why did the farmer call his pig "Ink"?
*Because it was always running out of the pen.*

........................................

Why shouldn't you tell a secret to a pig?
*He's a squealer.*

# Rabbits

What's the difference between a counterfeit dollar and a crazy rabbit?
*One is bad money and the other is a mad bunny.*

......................................................

Carry a rabbit in a storm, and the wind will blow the hare in your face.

......................................................

Mike: "I just read that somewhere there's a rabbit giving birth every second."

Ted: "Wow! Somebody should find her and stop her!"

Why was the rabbit so unhappy?
*She was having a bad hare day.*

What do you get when you cross a bunny rabbit with the World Wide Web?
*A Hare Net.*

What's the difference between a bunny and a lumberjack?
*One chews and hops, the other hews and chops.*

How do you find a lost rabbit?
*Make a noise like a carrot.*

How do you catch a unique rabbit?
*Unique up on it.*
How do you catch a tame rabbit?
*Tame way. Unique up on it!*

What did the pink rabbit say to the blue rabbit?
*"Cheer up!"*

How can you tell when it's rabbit pie for dinner?

*It has hares in it.*

How do you get if you pour boiling water down rabbit holes?

*Hot, cross bunnies!*

What is a twip?

*A twip is what a wabbit takes when he wides a twain.*

How do you know that carrots are good for your eyesight?

*Have you ever seen a rabbit with glasses?*

What do you have if there are one hundred rabbits standing in a row and ninety-nine take a step back?

*A receding hare line.*

# Skunks

Two little skunks, one named In and one named Out, wanted to go play. Their parents told them they could, but an hour later, only Out came back.

"Hasn't In come in?" asked Father Skunk.

"Out went out with In, but only Out came back in," said Mother Skunk.

"Well, Out," said Father, "you better go out and find In and bring her in."

So Out did. And only a few

moments later, he returned with his wayward sister.

"Ah, good," said Mother Skunk, pleased. "How did you find her?"

Out smiled. "Instinct," he said.

..................................................

How do you keep a skunk from smelling?

*Hold its nose.*

..................................................

Why shouldn't you shortchange a skunk?

*Because he's bound to make a stink.*

..................................................

What did the judge say when the skunk came in to testify?

*"Odor in the court!"*

..................................................

"Look over there!" said the frightened skunk to his pal. "There's a human with a gun, and he's getting closer and closer! What are we going to do?"

The second skunk knelt down and replied, "Let us spray. . . ."

# Snails

What was the snail doing on the highway?

*About one mile a day.*

How do snails get their shells all shiny?

*They use snail polish.*

What animal is the strongest?

*A snail. He carries his house.*

A snail starts a slow climb up the trunk of an apple tree. A sparrow observing his progress can't help laughing and says, "Don't you know

there aren't any apples on the
tree yet?"

"Yes," said the snail, "but there will
be by the time I get up there."

.....................................................

A snail goes into a car dealership.
She asks the salesman if they sell red
convertibles. The salesman answers,
"Yes. But do you have a valid license
and the finances to pay for the car?"

The snail replies, "Yes, I have
both. But I will only buy the car on
one condition—that you have a big
S painted on the side." The salesman
ponders that for a moment. It seems
odd to him, but it isn't every day that
he sells an expensive convertible, so
he agrees.

A few weeks later, the car is all
ready, and the salesman calls the
snail to tell her she can come pick it
up. The snail is really pleased with her
car and thanks the salesman warmly.

The man is curious about the big S
on the car, so he asks, "Why did you

want that letter painted on the convertible?"

The snail replies, "When I drive by, I want everyone to say, 'Look at that S car go!' "

# Snakes

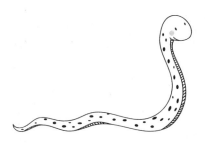

What do you call a snake that drinks too much coffee?

A hyper viper.

.......................................

Son: "I have good news and bad news."

Mom: "What's the good news?"

Son: "I captured a snake as long as the bathtub."

Mom: "What's the bad news?"

Son: "It just escaped from the bathtub."

.......................................

What do snakes do after an argument?

*They hiss and make up.*

What would you get if you crossed an eight-foot snake with a five-foot snake?

*Nothing. Snakes don't have feet.*

......................................................

A man was driving down a lonely country road when heavy snow began to fall. His windows fogged up, and his wiper blades were very badly worn and soon fell apart. When the visibility was so poor that the man couldn't see out of the front of his car anymore, he stopped the car. Then he got out and started to turn over large rocks. The search resulted in him finding two frozen snakes. The man straightened the snakes out and stuck them flat onto his blades, and they worked just fine.

Haven't you ever heard of "wind-chilled vipers"?

......................................................

Why is it so hard to fool a snake?

*Because you can't pull its leg.*

Baby Snake: "Mom, are we poisonous?"

Mommy Snake: "We most certainly are! Why?"

Baby Snake: "I just bit my tongue!"

..................................................

How can you tell if a snake enjoyed a good joke?

*He laughs hiss-terically.*

..................................................

What school subjects are snakes best at?

*Hiss-tory.*

..................................................

What kind of snake is good at math?

*An adder.*

# Turkeys

Why did the turkey cross the road?
*It was the chicken's day off.*

.......................................................

What did the turkey with a sore throat say?
*"Gargle, gargle, gargle."*

.......................................................

What did the turkey with a sore leg say?
*"Hobble, hobble, hobble."*

.......................................................

What does a turkey that argues a lot say?
*"Squabble, squabble, squabble."*

What did the dizzy turkey say?

*Nothing. He just went wobble, wobble, wobble.*

......................................................

Just before Thanksgiving, the teacher asked her kindergarten class, "What do you have to be thankful for?"

One youngster answered, "I'm thankful I'm not a turkey!"

......................................................

Why did they let the turkey join the band?

*Because he had his own drumsticks.*

# Turtles

What was the turtle doing on the highway?

*About one mile an hour.*

.....................................................

Two turtles were slowly moving down the road when one was struck in the head by a falling coconut. His friend, afraid that the turtle had lost his memory, rushed his injured companion to the emergency room.

The next day, the friend asked to speak with the doctor. "How is his memory?" asked the concerned friend.

"He's better," responded the

doctor. "In fact, I'm happy to tell you that he has turtle recall."

..................................................

Why did the turtle cross the road?
*To get to the Shell station.*

..................................................

Three turtles—Norm, Sonny, and Bart—decide to go on a picnic. Norm packs the picnic basket with cookies, drinks, and sandwiches. The picnic site they've chosen is ten miles away, and it takes the turtles ten days to get there. By the time they arrive, all three turtles are exhausted. Norm unloads each item from the basket. He takes out the sodas and says, "Sonny, please give me the bottle opener."

"I didn't bring the bottle opener," Sonny says. "I thought you packed it."

Norm gets worried. He turns to Bart. "Bart, do you have the bottle opener?"

Naturally, Bart doesn't have it, so the turtles are ten miles away from their home without soda. Norm and Sonny plead with Bart to return home and retrieve it, but Bart refuses, knowing that the two turtles will eat all of the food by the time he gets back. Somehow, after about two hours of begging, the turtles manage to convince Bart to go, promising that they won't touch the food.

So Bart sets off down the road, slowly and steadily. Twenty days pass, but Bart has not returned. Norm and Sonny are confused and hungry, but a promise is a promise. Another day passes, and still no Bart, but a promise is a promise. After three more days pass without Bart in sight, Norm starts getting restless. "I need food!" he cries.

"No!" Sonny retorts. "We promised." Five more days pass. Sonny realizes that Bart probably stopped at the Burger King down the road, so the two turtles weakly lift the lid, get a sandwich, and prepare to eat their meal.

Suddenly, Bart pops out from behind a rock and says, "Just for that, I'm not going."

......................................

A man went to the store to buy a container of Turtle Wax for his car. When he got to the store, he realized how much the wax cost, and he asked, "Why is Turtle Wax so expensive?"

The clerk replied, "Because they have such tiny ears."

......................................

The psychiatrist was surprised to see a tortoise come into his office. "What can I do for you, Mr. Tortoise?" asked the psychiatrist.

"I'm terribly shy, Doctor," answered the tortoise. "I want to be cured."

"No problem. Hopefully I can soon have you out of your shell."

# Zebras

What's black and white and red all over?

*A blushing zebra.*

What's black and white, black and white, black and white, and green?

*Three zebras fighting over a pickle.*

What has stripes and goes around and around?

*A zebra in a revolving door.*

What's black and white and makes a lot of noise?

*A zebra with a set of drums.*

# More Animals

Why were the squirrels sent to the principal's office?

*Because they drove the teacher nuts.*

..................................................

What did one mule say to the other mule?

*"I get a kick out of you."*

..................................................

What do rhinoceroses have that no other animal has?

*Baby rhinoceroses.*

..................................................

Two buffalo were grazing contentedly on the open prairie when a cowboy rode up. Looking at the animals, he shook his head and said, "You two are the worst-looking buffalo I ever saw. Your fur is tangled, you have bumps on your backs, and you slobber all over the place."

As the cowboy rode off, the first buffalo said to the second, "I think I just heard a discouraging word."

..................................................

What's worse than looking into the eye of a great white shark?

*Looking into his tonsils.*

..................................................

What does a chipmunk get when it rains?

*It gets wet.*

..................................................

What do you call two spiders that just married?

*Newlywebs.*

..................................................

What did the mother buffalo say to her son before he left?

*Bison.*

What did the beaver say to the tree?
*"It's been nice gnawing you."*

What is the best way to catch
a squirrel?
*Climb a tree and act like a nut.*

What is a shark's favorite game?
*Swallow the leader.*

A little boy returned from grocery shopping with his mom. While his mother put away the groceries, the little boy opened his box of animal crackers and spread them out all over the kitchen table.

"What are you doing?" asked his mom.

"The box says you shouldn't eat them if the seal is broken," said the little boy. "I'm looking for the seal."

What is the best advice to give
a worm?
*Sleep late!*

Camel 1: "How is life treating you?"
    Camel 2: "I've had hard times, but I'm finally getting over the hump."

......................................................

Why did the spider buy a car?
    *So he could take it out for a spin.*

......................................................

What did the baby porcupine say when it backed into the cactus?
    *"Is that you, Mother?"*

......................................................

What do you get when you cross a robber and a shark?
    *A bite out of crime.*

......................................................

What do you get if you cross a sheep and a rainstorm?
    *A wet blanket.*

......................................................

What do llamas like to eat?
    *Llama beans.*

......................................................

Why did the ram fall over the cliff?
    *He didn't see the ewe turn.*

Two friends went hunting for moose in Canada every year. Each time they were flown out to the marshland in a small bush airplane.

After landing them at their site, the pilot said, "I'll be back to pick you up in five days, and you can only return with you two, your gear, and one moose."

In five days when the pilot landed to pick them up, he found that the men had two moose. He was livid. "I told you only one moose! It's impossible to fly out with the weight of two."

The men said, "But we were here last year, and that pilot took us with two moose, so we thought maybe you could too."

The pilot said, "I'm the best pilot in this country, so if he can do it, I can too."

They stuffed everything into the small plane, closed the door, and took off. They made it up fine, until they came to a tree at the end of the runway and suddenly crashed right into the top of it. Moose, gear, and men went in all directions. When one of the hunters came to, he looked around and said, "Max, where are we?"

The other said, "I'm not sure, Frank, but it's about 150 yards farther than we got last year."

........................................

A Sunday school class was discussing the story the teacher had just read. "What can we learn from the story of Jonah and the whale?" the teacher asked.

One of the children answered, "What we learned is that people make whales sick."

........................................

What is brown, has four feet and a hump, and is found in Alaska?
*A lost camel.*

What did the daddy hedgehog say to his son just before he spanked him?

*"This is going to hurt me far more than it will hurt you."*

What animal is always laughing?

*A happy-potamus.*

Why do white sheep eat more grass than black sheep?

*Because there are more of them.*

Why are dolphins more clever than humans?

*Within three hours they can train a person to stand beside a pool and feed them fish.*

What do you call a camel with no hump?

*Humphrey.*

A panda bear walked into a restaurant and ordered a sandwich. When he received the sandwich, he ate it and then took out a gun, shot a hole in the ceiling, and left the restaurant.

A policeman caught up with the panda and told him he had broken the law. The panda bear told the policeman that he was innocent and, if he didn't believe him, to look in the encyclopedia. The policeman got a reference book and looked up "panda bear."

The entry read, "Panda Bear: Eats shoots and leaves."

......................................

The manager of a large city zoo was composing a letter to order a pair of animals. He sat at his computer and typed, "I would like to order two mongooses, to be delivered at your earliest convenience."

He stared at the screen, focusing on the odd-looking word *mongooses*. Then he deleted the word and added another, so that the sentence now read: "I would like to place an order for two mongeese, to be delivered at your earliest convenience."

Once more he stared at the screen, this time analyzing the new word, which seemed just as strange as the original one. Finally, he deleted the whole sentence and started all over.

"Everyone knows no zoo should be without a mongoose," he typed. "Please send us two of them."

# Menagerie

What would you get if you crossed a parrot with an elephant?

*An animal that tells you everything it remembers.*

..................................................

A farmer went out to the barn to milk his cow early in the morning. He was milking away quietly and had the bucket almost half-full when a fly flew into the barn and started circling around his head. Suddenly, the fly flew into the cow's ear. The farmer didn't think much about it until the fly squirted out into his bucket.

Looks like it went in one ear and out the udder.

What is worse than a centipede with sore feet?

*A giraffe with a sore throat.*

What is worse than a giraffe with a sore throat?

*An alligator with a toothache.*

What is worse than an alligator with a toothache?

*A turtle with claustrophobia.*

.................................................

Two men were fishing in stormy weather. They suddenly were thrown off the boat and found themselves in rough water, with sharks swimming around them. As the sharks began to argue over which got their pick of the fishermen, the largest shark swam over and offered to help them. "I'll help you out," said the shark. "But it's going to cost you an arm and a leg."

.................................................

Two men went duck hunting with their dogs, but without success. "I've figured out what we're doing wrong," said the first one.

"What's that?" asked the second.

"We're not throwing the dogs high enough!"

................................................

What animal can jump higher than the great pyramids?

*Any animal—pyramids can't jump.*

................................................

A man brought a rabbit, a frog, and a chicken to a talent agent's office. As the agent watched with indifference, the frog drank from a glass of water while the rabbit danced around the chicken and performed somersaults.

Just as the agent was about to tell the man to take his animals and leave, the rabbit bowed and said, "Thank you and good night!"

"That's amazing!" said the agent. "The rabbit is hired."

"But what about the frog?" asked the man.

"The frog doesn't have any talent; I want the rabbit," replied the agent.

"But the chicken—" he began.

"No chicken, I want the rabbit only!" the agent insisted.

The following week the agent got the rabbit an appearance on a TV variety show. When it was introduced, the rabbit hopped onto the stage, cleared its throat, and then silently walked off.

"What happened?" the agent asked the owner. "The rabbit didn't say a word!"

"No," said the owner. "The rabbit doesn't talk."

"But last week in my office I heard it—"

"I was trying to tell you."

"Tell me what?"

"About the chicken. He's a ventriloquist."

........................................

Hank decided to call his dog Stripe. His friend Dan looked at him like he was crazy. "Why did you call your dog Stripe?" asked Dan. "He's a dalmatian with black spots."

"Well, my other pet is named Spot," explained Hank.

"You didn't tell me you had another dalmatian," said Dan.

"I don't. My other pet is a zebra."

......................................

Why do kings have royal seals?
*Because royal walruses eat too much.*

......................................

A tourist was fishing off the coast of Florida when his boat capsized. He could swim, but he was afraid there might be alligators, so he hung on to the side of the overturned boat. Spotting an old beachcomber standing on the shore, the tourist called, "Are there any alligators around here?"

"Nah," the man hollered back. "They haven't been around here for years!"

Feeling safe, the tourist began swimming toward shore. About halfway there, he asked the guy, "How'd they get rid of the gators?"

"They didn't do anything," answered the beachcomber. "The sharks got 'em all."

.................................................

A turtle was mugged by three snails, but when the police asked the turtle to give a description of what happened, all he could say was "I don't know, Officer. It just all happened so fast!"

.................................................

Mrs. White and Mrs. Carter were discussing their children's sleeping habits. "I have trouble getting Willy up in the morning," said Mrs. White.

"Oh, that isn't a problem for me," replied Mrs. Carter. When it's time for Stu to get up, I put the cat in his bed."

"How does that get him up?" asked Mrs. White.

"Well," said Mrs. Carter, "he sleeps with the dog."

What do you call a mouse that hangs out with a bunch of pythons?
  *Lunch.*

..................................................

What did the dog do after he swallowed a firefly?
  *He barked with de-light!*

..................................................

What did the termite do when she couldn't carry the twig on her own?
  *She hired an assist-ant.*

..................................................

What do you call the second bird that's been eaten by the same cat?
  *An after-dinner tweet.*

..................................................

What do you get when you cross an elephant with a kangaroo?
  *Big holes all over Australia.*

..................................................

Boy: "Sir, could you sell me a shark?"
  Pet Shop Owner: "What would you do with a shark?"
Boy: "The cat's trying to eat my goldfish, and I want to teach him a lesson."

What do you call a bird that's been eaten by a cat?

*A swallow.*

......................................................

A man was riding his horse down a bridle path when a dog walking down the path said, "Hello."

Surprised, the man said, "I didn't know dogs could talk!"

The horse said, "Neither did I."

......................................................

A man runs into the vet's office carrying his dog, yelling for help. He is rushed back to an examination room and puts his dog down on the table. The vet examines the still, limp body and after a few minutes tells the man that his dog, unfortunately, is dead.

The man is clearly troubled and not willing to accept this, so he demands a second opinion. The vet goes into the back room and returns with a cat and puts the cat down beside the dog's body. The cat sniffs the dog, walks from head to tail poking and sniffing the body, and finally looks at the vet and meows. The vet says to the man, "I'm sorry, but the cat thinks that your dog is dead too."

The man is still unwilling to accept that his dog is gone. The vet brings in a Black Labrador. The Lab sniffs the body, walks from head to tail, and looks at the vet and barks. The vet looks at the man and says, "I am so sorry, but the Lab thinks your dog is dead too."

The man, finally resigned to the diagnosis, thanks the vet and asks how much he owes. The vet answers, "Four hundred and fifty dollars."

"Four hundred and fifty dollars to tell me that my dog is dead?" shouted the man.

"Well," the vet replied, "it would have been only fifty dollars for my initial diagnosis. The additional four hundred dollars was for the cat scan and lab work."

What do you get when you cross a hen with a hyena?

*An animal that laughs at every yolk.*

..................................................

Timmy was in the garden filling in a hole when his neighbor peered over the fence. Intrigued with what the young boy was up to, he politely asked, "What are you up to there, Timmy?"

"My goldfish died," said Tim tearfully, without looking up, "and I've just buried him."

The neighbor was concerned. "That's an awfully big hole for a goldfish, isn't it?"

Timmy pressed down on the top of the mound then replied, "That's because he's inside your cat."

..................................................

What do you get when you cross a parrot with a pig?

*A bird that hogs the conversation.*

What do you get if you cross a centipede and a parrot?

*A walkie-talkie.*

......................................

What is the difference between a fly and a bird?

*A bird can fly but a fly can't bird.*

......................................

What do you get if you cross a parrot with a cat?

*A carrot.*

......................................

What's better than a dog that can count?

*A spelling bee.*

......................................

What did the toad say after listening to one of the rabbit's jokes?

*"You croak me up."*

......................................

How do you spell *mousetrap* using three letters?

*C-A-T.*

......................................

What three keys can't open a door?

*A turkey, a monkey, and a donkey.*

How do you know that owls are more clever than chickens?

*Have you ever heard of Kentucky Fried Owl?*

..................................................

What's the difference between a coyote and a flea?

*One howls on the prairie, and the other prowls on the hairy.*

..................................................

What do you get if you cross a cow and a camel?

*Lumpy milk shakes.*

..................................................

What do you get if you cross a cow with a mule?

*Milk with a kick.*

..................................................

Did you hear about the man who tried to cross a lion with a goat?

*He had to get a new goat.*

..................................................

A workman had just finished laying a carpet in a house when he realized he had lost half of his sandwich.

Looking around, he saw a lump under the carpet. Not wanting to pull the carpet up again, he just got out his hammer and smashed the lump flat.

As he was cleaning up, the lady came in. "You've done a great job here! Just one thing, though: Have you seen our pet frog anywhere?"

......................................................

What do you get if you cross a worm with an elephant?

*Big holes in your garden.*

......................................................

One day a mime was visiting the zoo and attempted to earn some money as a street performer. But as soon as he started to draw a crowd, the zookeeper seized him and dragged him into his office. Rather than telling the mime not to perform on zoo property, however, the zookeeper reported that the zoo's most popular attraction, a gorilla, had passed away and the keeper feared that attendance at the zoo would decline. He asked the mime if he would be interested in employment, dressing up as the gorilla until they could find another one. The mime pondered the offer and accepted.

The following morning, he donned the gorilla suit and climbed into the cage before the zoo opened. When the crowds began to gather, the mime found that he'd stumbled onto an incredible job opportunity. He was able to sleep all he wanted, play all day, and make fun of people. The crowds were much bigger than they ever had been when he was a mime.

Before long though, the crowds began to tire of him, and he became bored just swinging on the trees in his cage. He discovered that the visitors were paying more attention to the lion in the next cage. Not wanting to lose his status as the zoo's most popular attraction, he climbed to the top of his cage, crawled across the partition, and hung from the top of the lion's cage. Of course, this enraged the lion, but the crowd loved it.

This practice went on for some time. The mime in the gorilla suit kept teasing the lion, the lion kept roaring, the crowds grew larger, and the mime's income kept increasing. Then, one horrible day, as he was hanging above the furious lion, the mime lost his grip and fell.

The mime found himself face-to-face with the lion, which prepared to pounce. The mime was so terrified that he began to run around the cage with the lion following close behind. The crowd roared its approval.

At last, the lion caught up to the gorilla and pounced. The mime found himself on his back, looking up at the irate lion, and began yelling, "Help me!"

Immediately, the lion placed his paw over the mime's mouth and said, "Be quiet! What are you trying to do, get us both fired?"

"Ask me if I am a tiger."

"Are you a tiger?"

"Yup. Okay, ask me if I am a kitten."

"Are you a kitten?"

"No, I just told you I am a tiger!"

......................................................

What game do ants play with elephants?

*Squash.*

......................................................

What do you get when you cross a rhinoceros with a blackbird?

*A lot of broken telephone poles.*

......................................................

A duck hunter was looking to purchase a new bird dog. When he found a dog that was able to walk on water to retrieve a duck, he knew he had to look no further. He was certain that none of his friends would ever believe in his new dog's abilities, so he decided to break the news to a cynical friend of his by taking the man hunting.

On the shore of the lake, a flock

of ducks flew by. The dog's new owner fired, and one duck fell. The dog responded by jumping onto the water. He proudly trotted across the lake to retrieve the bird, only getting his paws wet.

The skeptical friend watched the demonstration but didn't say a word.

Later, as they were driving home, the hunter asked his friend, "Did you happen to notice anything unusual about my new dog?"

"Of course," said the friend. "He can't swim."

......................................

What do you get when you cross a giraffe with a hedgehog?

*A six-foot toothbrush.*

......................................

Three animals were having a disagreement over who was the best: The first, a hawk, claimed that because of his ability to fly, he was able to attack anything repeatedly from above, and his prey didn't have a chance. The second, a lion, based his claim on his strength—none in the forest dared to challenge him. The third, a skunk, insisted he did not need either flight or strength to ward off any creature. As the trio argued, a grizzly bear came along and swallowed them all: hawk, lion, and stinker!

..................................................

What do you get when you cross a mink with a kangaroo?
*A fur coat with very large pockets.*

..................................................

A lion woke up one morning feeling rather meaner than usual. He set out and cornered a small monkey and roared, "Who is mightiest of all jungle animals?"

The fearful monkey said, "You are, mighty lion!"

Later in the day, the lion faced a wild beast and fiercely bellowed, "Who is the mightiest of all jungle animals?"

The terrified wild beast replied, "Oh great lion, you are by far the mightiest animal in the jungle!"

With his air of superiority, the lion strutted up to an elephant and roared, "Who is mightiest of all jungle animals?"

In an instant, the elephant picked the lion up with his trunk and pounded him against a tree several times. The elephant then walked away.

The lion let out a moan of pain, lifted his head weakly, and yelled after the elephant, "Just because you don't know the answer, you don't have to get so upset about it!"

.................................................

A wealthy man decided to go on a safari in Africa. He took his beloved dog with him for company. One day the dog started chasing butterflies, and before long he found that he had gotten lost. He began to wander around and noticed that a leopard was quickly moving in his direction, obviously wanting to make a meal out of him.

The dog thought, *I'm in trouble now.* He then noticed some bones on the ground nearby and quickly settled down to gnaw on them with his back to the approaching cat.

Just as the leopard was about to pounce, the dog exclaimed loudly, "That certainly was a delicious leopard! I'll have to see if I can find any more around here."

Hearing this, the leopard stopped midstride as a look of terror came over him. He quickly ran away into the trees. "Whew," said the leopard. "That was too close. That dog nearly got me!"

Meanwhile, a monkey had been viewing the whole scene from a nearby tree. He figured he could use this knowledge, trading it for protection from the leopard. So he set off to find the leopard. But the dog saw him heading after the leopard with great speed and figured that something must be up.

The monkey soon found the leopard, told him everything, and made a deal with the leopard. The big cat was angry at being made a fool of and said, "Here, monkey, jump onto my back and see what'll happen to that scheming dog."

The dog saw the leopard coming with the monkey on his back and thought to himself, *What am I going to do now?* But rather than running away, the dog sat down with his back to his attackers, acting as if he didn't know that they were there. Just as they got close enough to hear, the dog said, "Where can that monkey be? I can't trust him! He left an hour ago to find me another leopard, and he still isn't back!"

........................................

What do you get if you cross a leopard with a watchdog?

*A terrified postman.*

How do you know if your cat has eaten a duckling?

*She's got that down-in-the-mouth look.*

..............................................

Hired by a zoo to bring them some baboons, the big-game hunter came up with a scheme to trap them—the only supplies he needed were a sack, a gun, and a vicious dog.

He went into the jungle with his assistant, and after several days they finally found a large number of baboons. "This is the plan," he explained to his assistant. "I'll climb this tree and shake the tree—if there are any baboons up there, they will fall from the branches to the ground. The dog will bite their tails and immobilize them so that you can pick them up safely and put them in the sack."

"Well, what do I need a gun for?" asked the assistant.

"If I fall out of the tree, shoot the dog!"

Why did the cat frown when she passed the henhouse?

*Because she heard fowl language.*

..................................................

What did the cat do when he swallowed some cheese?

*He waited by the mouse hole with baited breath.*

..................................................

What did the cowboy say when the bear ate Lassie?

*"Well, doggone."*

..................................................

What happens when it rains cats and dogs?

*You can step in a poodle.*

..................................................

What do you get if you cross a rottweiler and a hyena?

*I don't know, but I'll join in if it laughs.*

..................................................

What do you get if you cross a skunk with a bear?

*Winnie the Phew.*

A kangaroo kept getting out of his pen at the zoo. Knowing that he could hop high, the zoo officials decided to put up a ten-foot fence. He was out the next morning, just hopping around the zoo.

A twenty-foot fence was put up. Again he escaped.

When the fence was thirty feet high, a camel in the next pen asked the kangaroo, "How high do you think they'll go?"

The kangaroo replied, "About a thousand feet unless somebody starts locking the gate at night!"

..................................................

If you were surrounded by thirty lions, twenty-five elephants, and ten hippos, how would you get away from them?

*Get off the merry-go-round.*

How do you get down off an elephant?

> *You can't—you get down off a goose.*

# Noah and the Animals

Why did some snakes disobey Noah when he said, "Go forth and multiply"?
*They couldn't—they were adders!*

......................................................

What was Noah's profession?
*He was an ark-itect.*

......................................................

Who ran the first canning factory?
*Noah—he had a boatful of preserved pairs.*

Why didn't the two worms go into Noah's ark in an apple?

*Because everyone had to go in pairs.*

.................................................

Just before the ark set sail, Noah saw his two sons fishing over the side. "Go easy on the bait, guys," he said. "Remember I've only got two worms."

.................................................

As Noah and his family were disembarking from the ark, they paused on a ridge to look back. "We should have done something, Noah," his wife said. "That old hulk of an ark will sit there and be an eyesore on the landscape for years to come."

"Everything's taken care of," Noah assured her. "I left the two termites aboard."

.................................................

Where did Noah keep the bees?

*In the ark hives.*

Where was Noah when the lights went out?

*In d'ark.*

...................................................

What did Noah say as he was loading the ark?

*"Now I herd everything."*

...................................................

What kind of lighting did Noah use for the ark?

*Floodlights.*

...................................................

Was Noah the first one out of the ark?

*No, he came forth out of the ark.*

# Test Your Bible Smarts!

## *The World's Greatest Bible Trivia for Kids*

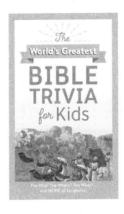

What's better than a fun book of Bible trivia? *The World's Greatest Bible Trivia for Kids!* You'll be challenged, entertained, and inspired by dozens of trivia quizzes on the who, the where, the what, and the MORE of scripture!

Paperback / 978-1-68322-772-4 / $4.99